ABOVE

ALL ELSE

60 DEVOTIONS

ABOVE
ALL ELSE

FOR YOUNG WOMEN

CHELSEA CROCKETT

ZONDERVAN®

ZONDERVAN

Above All Else
Copyright © 2019 by Beauty Licious, Inc.

Requests for information should be addressed to:
Zondervan, *3900 Sparks Dr. SE, Grand Rapids, Michigan 49546*

Hardcover ISBN 978-0-310-76726-8

Ebook ISBN 978-0-310-76730-5

Scripture quotations are taken from the Holy Bible, New International Version®, NIV®. Copyright © 1973, 1978, 1984, 2011 by Biblica, Inc.® Used by permission of Zondervan. All rights reserved worldwide. www.Zondervan.com. The "NIV" and "New International Version" are trademarks registered in the United States Patent and Trademark Office by Biblica, Inc.®

Any internet addresses (websites, blogs, etc.) and telephone numbers in this book are offered as a resource. They are not intended in any way to be or imply an endorsement by Zondervan, nor does Zondervan vouch for the content of these sites and numbers for the life of this book.

Interior design: Denise Froehlich

Printed in China

19 20 21 22 23 / DSC / 10 9 8 7 6 5 4 3 2 1

*This book is dedicated to those who
believe their best days are ahead
while walking with the Lord.*

CONTENTS

JORDAN LEE DOOLEY

I don't know about you, but I can get wrapped up in a lot of things that really don't matter. As an achiever, I struggle with overworking myself, worrying about how a project will get done, or even what others think of my performance.

While there's nothing wrong with being a hard worker, I've learned how unhealthy it can become when my focus gets caught up in things I can't take with me. When I don't take time to rest, when I put my work above all else, it reveals what I truly believe: that my performance, achievements, and work are what sustains me. I begin to rely on and prioritize the sense of accomplishment more than I rely on God in my life. That is an exhausting way to live. It's funny because I know it can be so easy to list out our priorities. Maybe your priorities look a little like this:

FAITH | FAMILY | FRIENDS | FITNESS

Okay, perhaps you've never done the alliteration thing like I did here—my list when I first learned how to make a Facebook profile. At the time, I thought it was pretty clever.

Though at this season in my life, I'd have to add another category: *Work*. (Unfortunately, that *W* really throws off the alliteration.) So here's my final, ideal list of priorities:

FAITH | FAMILY | FRIENDS | FITNESS AND WORK

Look at that list. It looks good, doesn't it? Makes complete sense, right? And in theory, it all looks great. But here's the thing about priorities: they're not meant to be listed, they're meant to be *lived*.

In other words, my ideal list—and your list—can look absolutely perfect on paper and be an absolute mess in practice.

When my focus on work, achievement, or the way I look or am perceived begins to take over, the way I'm actually investing my time, talent, energy, and resources does not add up to the way my list is laid out. Instead, my priorities begin to look more like:

WORK AND FITNESS | FAMILY | FRIENDS | FAITH

More often than not, what I'd like to SAY is my top priority gets put on the back burner day after day. No wonder I get anxious.

Sister, maybe work isn't what's hindering you, but something else is. Something you get so obsessed with and overwhelmed by that your priorities get all out of whack if you're not careful. Maybe, like me, what you achieve each day can begin to be placed above all else in your life. Or perhaps your boyfriend begins to sit above all else in your life. Or social media, or money, or how your hair looks, or if you have a thigh gap, or whatever you spend so much energy focusing on.

I don't know what issue has taken over your top spot, but no matter what it is, if you find you have a hard time actually living out the order you list your priorities, Chelsea Crockett's book won't only challenge you as you read, it will walk with you as you learn to actually put what matters most *Above All Else.*

Jordan Lee Dooley

INTRODUCTION

For years, I've wanted my friends, family, and everyone, really, to know God loves us deeply and wants to spend time with us. He desires to be with us much like we love spending time with the ones who make us happy. I was in high school when God first spoke to me about spending time with him. As I was praying that day, I heard his still, small voice say, "This is what I love, Chelsea. I love when you hang out with me." And y'all, I broke (not literally, but I sobbed hysterically). The way I approached my relationship with God was entirely different after that moment. My mindset shifted again when I was about eighteen years old. Until then, I hadn't recognized I didn't have to work my way to the Lord's love. I'd believed the lie that God wouldn't love me or want to be in a relationship with me unless I was "good" enough for him. The culture we live in sometimes promotes the falsehood we must prove we're worth spending time with—that we have to be kind enough, or beautiful enough, or smart enough for people to like us. Yet God, in his boundless love, is chasing after us in our weakness.

The Lord *adores* spending time with you. As much as we put pressure on ourselves to read, pray, and worship so we can check them off our mental "to-do" list, God delights in spending real, quality time with us. After these turning points in my life, God met me in ways I never dreamt. But one of the most transformative ways he's changed me is through his Word. The Bible has shaped the way I view and treat others because of God's mercy and the love he shows throughout time. The Word of God is so much more powerful than I'd given it credit for in the past. I used to glance at my Bible from across my room and want nothing to do with it. I found it boring, confusing, and, if I'm honest, uncomfortably convicting. There were times when I knew if I opened the pages of his Word, God's Holy Spirit would move me toward his heart, and that meant I would be encouraged to leave my selfish desires behind. But let me just tell you, friend, I am so glad his Word showed me that the more times I read it and apply what he says, the more I change for the better! I live for a purpose greater than myself and this world.

I've created this book to help you discover that, above all else, God wants a close and continuing relationship with each and every one of us. In *Above All Else*, we will be focusing on many situations, relationships, or transitional times in our lives by looking to Scripture as our guide. Each day, you'll be challenged to dive deeper on your own through writing, prayer, or reading to help you continue to grow in your faith. When interacting with this devotional, give yourself permission to ask questions about your faith, dig into the lies you may have believed at one point in your life, and allow Jesus to intervene in your story and speak his truth. The Bible is meant for all of us, and its purpose is to help us identify the voice of God in our lives. I'm so excited you've chosen to embark on this 60-day journey, and please know I am praying for growth, inspiration, and new beginnings for you.

XO,
Chels

DAY 1

KNOWN BY GOD

John 10:14–16

I am the good shepherd; I know my sheep and my sheep know me—just as the Father knows me and I know the Father—and I lay down my life for the sheep. I have other sheep that are not of this sheep pen. I must bring them also. They too will listen to my voice, and there shall be one flock and one shepherd.

You and I are more like sheep than we realize. Which is why Jesus intentionally refers to us as sheep in John 10. Sheep are some of the most defenseless animals on earth. For example, these fluffy guys will get dehydrated if they are not led to water, because they're totally unaware of their surroundings. The intriguing thing is that sheep have a natural desire to follow a shepherd. They can't do too many things without guidance.

Similarly, Jesus is our good shepherd. He leads us to all the places we need to go. Trusting his leadership means you may not know ahead of time all the places (both physical and emotional) you'll end up; it requires faith and trust that you'll be led where you need to be at the right time. When you stay close enough to God to hear his voice and listen to his guiding words, you also take the most important step toward loving God with all your heart and seeing his love for you. Trusting a leader is a much simpler choice when you have confidence that they know you inside and out. This is true with the God we serve. Since we are made in his image, and he made us himself, we can trust he knows what he's doing.

In the verse above, Jesus says he *knows* his sheep and his sheep know him, just as the Father knows him and he knows the Father. Whew. Read that line a few more times.

Just as intimately as the Lord knows his Son, he knows us! We are fully known by the God of the universe because we are his beloved creation. At the beginning of time, he saw the world and all that he had made, and he deemed it all "good," but he didn't call it "*very* good" until it included us.

TAKEAWAY: Let's position ourselves in a place where we are fully aware our God is closer to us than we can feel. When this is our mindset, we can stand before him in awe of the love he has for us and with a willingness to love him with our all in return.

CHALLENGE: Ask the Lord to change and shape you into the person you were created to be: someone who trusts in him for everything. It might not make sense to the world, but loving God with our all takes spending time with him. This doesn't always mean sitting on your bed in your room deciphering the Bible. Sometimes it's praying in the car, running in your neighborhood with awareness of the beauty around you, or taking a break from your phone and work to spend time with those you love. The more time you spend with him, the better you will know him as he knows you. Rest in him today, and he will draw near to you.

THOUGHTS:

DAY 2

LOVING OTHERS AS YOURSELF

Philippians 2:3–4

Do nothing out of selfish ambition or vain conceit. Rather, in humility value others above yourselves, not looking to your own interests but each of you to the interests of the others.

Over two hundred names are given to Jesus Christ throughout Scripture. One of the many names is "friend of sinners." When I was younger I found this incredibly weird. How can someone so perfect want to be friends with people who mess up all the time? If we are called to look and act more like Christ as we follow him, how are we supposed to balance being a friend to sinners while still obeying God's command to not sin?

Jesus lived with sinners, and everyone he encountered eventually sinned against him. But still, he chose to take on our sins and give us redemption. The reason we can value others above ourselves is due to the fact we know who we are in Christ (sinners who have been forgiven), and loving and serving others is a part of our mission on earth. If we all lend a hand to the person next to us, we all become a stronger force to share the love of God.

Jesus lived amongst sinners to serve them and look to their best interests (by ultimately saving them, and us). There are opportunities to help others all around us—we just have to be attentive to the opportunities we're given.

Before we help and serve others, though, it's important to know if we are spiritually healthy. The thoughts we take in are byproducts of the many images, voices, and examples we subscribe to, and they affect us in powerful ways. So to love others well and love from an overflow of our heart, we must take in things that are pure. To live life bigger than yourself is to treat others higher than yourself and to feed yourself the same gospel you share with those around you.

TAKEAWAY: A fulfilling life is one of selflessness. To serve others around us, we need to fill ourselves with the things of Jesus. It is natural (of our flesh) to want to serve ourselves all hours of the day, but when Christ enters the different parts of our lives, he gives us a new heart that is specifically oriented toward serving and being kind to others. Walk in the Spirit today, and remember there are opportunities all around you to make a heavenly impact.

CHALLENGE: Philippians is a great book about the church, our mission, and how saturating ourselves in the Lord's love is important. I encourage you to take time to walk chapter by chapter through this book. Today, start with chapter 1. Write down any words that speak to you. You'll be amazed how keeping verses close to your heart affects the way you treat people!

THOUGHTS:

GOD'S GREAT LOVE FOR US

Psalm 102:25–26

In the beginning you laid the foundations of the earth, and the heavens are the work of your hands. They will perish, but you remain; they will all wear out like a garment. Like clothing you will change them and they will be discarded.

Many of us spend time feeling like we are not who we need to be. We often compare ourselves to other people and assume something is wrong with us. I have a hard time with comparing my success to that of people who are more successful (or so it seems). When instead, what I really need to be focusing on during these times of self-doubt is something I've been told since I was a little girl: that I am loved unconditionally. Today's verse says that God "remains." If he remains when things around me are either fleeting or failing, his love will remain too. That reminder comforts me and gives me hope for the future.

God's incredible love for us is evidenced by his Son's sacrifice on the cross. Jesus came down to earth in relatable human form to put sin in its grave so we can live in relationship with God. In our struggle with comparison and distraction in this world, his sacrifice also shows us that his love is unconditional. If the world's population was only one human, he would die just for them. That fact blows my mind!

Our relationship with God should be based on our trust in God's radical love for and acceptance of us. The enemy wants us to focus on what is flawed within ourselves. That's because fixation on our flaws can easily become a sort of idol, causing our gaze to move off Jesus and onto the earthly view of ourselves instead. But when we know we are accepted and loved even in our imperfection, it's such a relief. God's unconditional love gives us confidence, boldness, and fearlessness.

TAKEAWAY: It's one thing to know in our minds that God loves us unconditionally, but it's another to believe it deep in our hearts. What we think, read, and see influences what we believe. Are you making a conscious effort to be in places and around people that influence you in a godly way? Scripture promises that if we want more God in our lives, he will reveal himself in incredible ways, but we also need to make sure we put more God in our lives ourselves as well.

CHALLENGE: When you go to bed at night, say to yourself, "God loves me unconditionally, and through faith I am made right in his eyes." Add this power to your life and meditate on God's promises.

THOUGHTS:

DAY 4

REST

Mark 6:31–32

*Then, because so many people were coming
and going that they did not even have a chance
to eat, he said to them, "Come with me by
yourselves to a quiet place and get some rest."
So they went away by themselves in a boat to a
solitary place.*

The world promotes a fast-paced, work-hard mentality. This mentality isn't necessarily a bad thing, but when busyness becomes an idol, it can become draining. We were designed to be human *beings*, not human doings. Resting is something Jesus did when he walked the earth. It's what God did on the seventh day after creating the world! If God himself rests, imagine how much we need rest as imperfect beings created in his image.

True rest that nourishes the soul doesn't come easily to most of us; you need to intentionally give yourself the rest you require. But while taking occasional time away from media and other distractions is important, it isn't enough; our only true, satisfying rest comes from following Christ's example. When the disciples returned from their mission of sharing the gospel to different areas and people, Jesus took them away to recharge. Doing God's work is important, but Jesus recognized that to do it effectively, we need periodic rest and renewal of our entire selves.

I've discovered anything that could potentially change the direction of someone's life takes a lot of effort, and doing so can be tiring but rewarding. For example, working out never "fits" into my day. It seems like there's always something else I could be doing or focusing on, but I carve out time in the day to give my body the exercise it needs. Similarly, making the time and space to rest your body, mind, and spirit is essential to living your best life on earth. To rest all three, I love finding a quiet place in nature to pray and talk with Jesus.

And resting isn't just important for *our* lives. To serve others well and do what we are called to do, we must take periodic breaks from working or helping others. A counselor I saw for a couple months gave me great perspective on rest, using the metaphor of a car tire. Before I started seeing her, I was not eating right or sleeping much. In essence, I was trying to move through life with a flat tire. I had healthy relationships, my work and career were going great, but because I was so focused on my relationships and outside needs, I wasn't taking care of my physical health—my life was out of balance, and I was drained. It took time to get back to a healthy lifestyle, and resting was a big part of it. Doing too much eventually leads to not being able to do anything at all. As the saying goes, "You can't pour from an empty cup." Resting is crucial to refilling your own reserves in order to better serve others. Setting up a regular schedule that incorporates rest is also a critical part of deepening your walk with the Lord and letting him take the lead.

TAKEAWAY: It is healthy to take a respite from the "grind" of work and life. Are you running on a flat tire due to lack of rest? You may need to change up some things. This could include taking a break from social media, making time for friends and family who support you, putting good foods into your body, and getting a full night's sleep. These may seem like pretty straightforward recommendations—and they are—but in our world, it's easy to lose sight of the simplest ways to take care of ourselves.

CHALLENGE: It does make it *easier* to love others when we are well-rested, well-fed, and comfortable, but the love we pour out comes from the cup of Christ and is without limit. Even on our days when we find it hard to serve, Christ is sufficient. To make room for growth, set aside a portion of your day to do something that fills your soul. Take a walk, turn off your phone an hour before bed so you can read, and write out your thoughts/prayers for the day!

THOUGHTS:

DAY 5

PRAYER

Matthew 21:22

If you believe, you will receive whatever you ask for in prayer.

I t's not always easy to believe that God is going to come through in the ways you hope he will. Oftentimes, he responds in a completely different way than what I've requested of him in prayer. I'm also ashamed to recall all the times I've said mindless words to get my prayer "in" for the day, expecting that God is like a drive-up window where my order will be filled no matter what I ask for.

It's important to remember that making all our requests known to the Lord is only a portion of what our prayer lives should look like. He knows our hearts and desires before we even ask! Prayer is also about growing our faith in and understanding of God. If we believe in our prayers by asking through faith, we will receive what we ask in some way if it furthers his kingdom. He is all-knowing, but as humans, our knowledge only goes so far. We may think we know what is best, but our perspective is not his. Therefore, it is important to pray for the will of God to unfold. He will either give us what we desire, something even better, or something completely different, according to what is best for us and his kingdom.

What is gained when we pray? We gain humility when we send up requests to the Lord, knowing he is the author of what lies ahead for our lives. Control goes out the window because we are trusting God will make a way. Heavenly perspective is gained, and so is peace. When God is with us in our prayer lives, we partner with him to see heaven come down to earth. Our prayers become more "on earth as it is in heaven," and less about us!

TAKEAWAY: Prayer is a direct line of communication to the one who made you and me. If you are struggling to make communication a daily practice with God, tell him! There is also so much guidance on how to pray and what to pray in God's Word. A pastor or worship leader does not have a divine connection to God that you could never have. God is just as available to you as he is to the next person.

CHALLENGE: I challenge you to read more scripture about prayer. See 2 Chronicles 7:14, Matthew 26:39, James 4:3, and Jeremiah 29:12–14.

THOUGHTS:

DAY 6

READING
THE WORD

Jeremiah 29:13

You will seek me and find me when you seek me with all your heart.

The Bible was never meant to limit God; it was meant to reveal all that he is. A lot of Christians are guilty of treating the Word of God as something they can get to in their spare time. I've been guilty of this. Sometimes the intention of reading Scripture is to get the "good Christian thing to do" checked off the list. Spending time with the One who created all of us becomes something we squeeze in if we have time, rather than a part of our everyday lifestyle. I've been there, and maybe you have too.

If we want the Lord to speak to us, we must open Scripture. His Word is the way we see through a heavenly lens and set our eyes on what matters. It shapes and molds us into the people we are meant to be. One of the beautiful things about the Bible is that it isn't just a book. Since the words inside are the living Word of God, they will continue to change us from the inside out if we continue to soak them in. Our souls are thirsty for these words, more than we realize. Just like our body craves food for nourishment, our soul cries out for more of God, who made us.

John 1:1 says that the Word *is* God. If the Word is Jesus and Jesus is God in flesh, then we have all we need to start our journey of seeking! The stories, poems, and wisdom in Scripture are just as applicable today as they were when they were written. But the Bible's purpose is not just life advice. It is God's act of stretching out his love into our life, coming into our world, and walking around in the problems and joys we have right now! Both Jesus and the Bible that tells us his story are living forces in our lives, changing us in real time. The most beautiful story of redemption and relationship is alive and active for us to grab on to and take part in today!

TAKEAWAY: We cannot get to know more of God or be molded into our best selves unless we regularly dive into a conversation with him. He so desperately wants to spend time with us, but he will never force his way into our lives.

CHALLENGE: Start studying one book of the Bible at a time. I have included an appendix at the back of the book with a list of different topical Bible studies. If you needed someone or something to remind you just how important God's Word is for everyday living, this is your sign!

THOUGHTS:

DAY 7

LIVING OUT
YOUR FAITH

John 11:39–40

"Take away the stone," he said. "But, Lord," said Martha, the sister of the dead man, "by this time there is a bad odor, for he has been there four days." Then Jesus said, "Did I not tell you that if you believe, you will see the glory of God?"

What does it look like to live out your faith so purposefully that it's evident to everyone you meet that you're a follower of Jesus? Have you ever met a person who is so intentional about their faith that it's contagious? A YouTuber that I follow named Emma Mae Jenkins has joy that is so radiant, I just want to be that joyful as well!

God wants that type of life for us because we were designed to live a life that is fulfilling. But we all have strengths and weaknesses, and sometimes our faith feels weakest when we need it most. When we go through hard things, our faith can feel as tired and frail as the other parts of us. But how incredible is it that we can delight in our weaknesses because Christ's name can be magnified in them? (See 2 Corinthians 12:9.) Some of my moments that could have been my weakest turned out to be my strongest because I had faith in God to lead me through.

I'm not sure where you currently are in your life, but it's important that we live out our faith no matter what we're facing. Earth is temporary, our feelings and situations are temporary, but God's faithfulness lasts forever. When the hurts and burdens of life are weighing you down, he is closer than you know. When you're confused, submit your questions to him first and then surround yourself with other believers. Even when life is great, continue to prioritize him and seek him with a thankful heart.

In John 11, when Jesus talks to Mary and Martha about their brother passing away, the sisters have faith that God is faithful no matter the circumstance in front of them. They were sad that their brother died (or so they thought), but hopeful they would see him again in eternity. If Jesus can raise dead people to life because of faith, imagine what else he can do!

TAKEAWAY: The key to living out your faith no matter what is staying so close to Jesus that you are walking hand in hand with him. We hear from him in his Word, through his living example, and via the Holy Spirit, who guides us in this life.

CHALLENGE: Most Christians waiver in their relationship with God because they don't think they need him in the "happy and successful" times of their lives. To thrive on this earth, we must be intentional about what we pursue in rough times and during exciting days. Today, I encourage you to read John 11, which talks about vibrant faith in Jesus that goes beyond what we imagine possible.

THOUGHTS:

DAY 8

KINDNESS

Galatians 5:22–26

But the fruit of the Spirit is love, joy, peace, forbearance, kindness, goodness, faithfulness, gentleness and self-control. Against such things there is no law. Those who belong to Christ Jesus have crucified the flesh with its passions and desires. Since we live by the Spirit, let us keep in step with the Spirit. Let us not become conceited, provoking and envying each other.

Kindness seems like a foreign attitude in today's world. I grew up thinking that everyone was kind and that all people had good intentions. As I got older, I realized everyone can be nice, but it is a choice to walk in kindness rather than judgment.

I love paying attention to kids and what they have to say, because I honestly believe I have a lot to learn from their simple view of life. I remember watching a video of a little boy who received a ton of toys for Christmas and was so excited to give them to kids he had never met. He wasn't being nice because he had to, he was being kind because he wanted to— giving to others was the most impactful thing he could think to do with all his blessings. This little boy inspired young people and adults to act in kindness toward those in need.

I imagine God looking on this little boy full of joy. There's a reason one of the fruits of the Spirit is kindness. Kind people are set apart from the world. Galatians tells us that kindness is a fruit we see from believers if they are walking with the Lord. Kindness goes hand in hand with the other fruits of the Spirit as well. You cannot have kindness without love, and joy without peace. They all work in harmony with one another. And they all come from the Spirit of God, overflowing into your life.

TAKEAWAY: Kindness is going the extra mile in a world where most don't give others the time of day. Choosing kindness is choosing to walk in the Spirit and not in the flesh.

CHALLENGE: Write out the fruits of the Spirit today and begin praying for growth in each one. Place your list somewhere you'll see it every day. If you do not have Galatians 5:22–23 memorized, I encourage you to do so!

THOUGHTS:

RIGHT CHOICE VS. EASY CHOICE

Matthew 7:13–14

*Enter through the narrow gate. For wide is
the gate and broad is the road that leads to
destruction, and many enter through it. But
small is the gate and narrow the road that leads
to life, and only a few find it.*

Life is full of choices. Sometimes the number of decisions we have to make in a day can feel overwhelming. But a beautiful part of living is having the ability to choose how we want to live. Some choose different paths than others, but we all are given options of how we want to live.

There are moments when big decisions are on the table, like the option to take the easy route or the right one. Maybe you have a decision or two to make right now and it's difficult to see which way to go. Whatever you face, every decision you make today influences the direction you head tomorrow.

Oftentimes, we focus too much on the big decisions we will make in the future and not enough on the small choices we need to make in our present. So how do we switch our focus? When we stop thinking so much about our future and start thinking of the present, our thoughts shift from "I wish" or "I should" to "I will" or "I am." That shift in words or thoughts changes us from being a victim of circumstance to being victorious over our own circumstances.

Centering yourself in Christ daily is essential to making the best decisions. For example, if you're in a place in a romantic relationship where you feel you will need to compromise boundaries and beliefs in order to move forward, deciding to stay in that relationship could lead to a lot of heartache. It can take courage to choose to walk toward what you know is wise, and sometimes it may not be the most exciting option. However, in a world where we are encouraged to show the excitement of our everyday lives, a still spirit that obeys Christ in the ordinary day to day is much more important than putting on a show for the world to see.

TAKEAWAY: Righteousness, and choosing the "right" path, is worth the extra effort it might take. By choosing this way of living—pursuing what the Lord has for us—we'll draw in the people we need in our lives, rather than those who lead us toward sinful ways.

CHALLENGE: Proverbs is a book of wisdom. If you want to be more versed in how to make the right choices, I encourage you to read the book of Proverbs. Let wisdom be close to you and watch your life and your decisions radically transform. To start, I recommend reading one proverb a day!

THOUGHTS:

CHOOSE TO BE BRAVE

1 Samuel 30:6

*David was greatly distressed because the men were talking of stoning him; each one was bitter in spirit because of his sons and daughters. But David found strength in the L*ORD *his God.*

When I hear the words *brave* or *courageous*, an image of a warrior comes to mind. Warriors know there is a battle to come, and they train ahead of time to prepare to fight their enemy. These extreme fighters know they will face opposition and intense situations that will stretch them, but they go into battle anyway. Warriors commit to and fight for what they believe in and will fight to the death for victory. As warriors for Christ, we can act with more courage than any fictional hero because we know we are on the side of good, justice, and love. Instead of hoping for a victory, we know the ultimate fight has already been won for us. And we can celebrate that victory because we're on the winning team.

But that doesn't mean we can stop training to fight. Our enemy (Satan) goes to battle every day for our hearts and minds. He can be desperate and ruthless because he knows he will be defeated in the end. His time and power to threaten, harm, and destroy us is limited, and he doesn't hold the keys to eternal life. Jesus made the permanent sacrifice for our sins on the cross. He won the war for us when he rose again, defeating death forever. He broke sin, death, and fear's power over us, and gave us the power of confidence in his strength and love. With these in our arsenal, we cannot be defeated.

In 1 Samuel 30, the Amalekites attacked and destroyed

the city of Ziklag with fire. Along with burning down the city where David and his army were staying, they also took all the women and children there captive. David was deeply sorrowful when he realized his family was taken, and upset when his men turned on him, but courageous because he knew how powerful his God was. He had confidence that justice would be served when he pursued the Amalekites with his four hundred men at his side. And David indeed recovered all that had been stolen from him and his men.

What if we tapped into the strength David had when people all around him were talking about stoning him to death? Our foe—be it sin or the enemy of death—has already been defeated on the cross. We can confidently pick up our swords and fight because we know our destination is in heaven with Jesus after our time on earth is up.

TAKEAWAY: In the Bible, the Word of God is said to be like a sharp two-edged sword. When we hold its wisdom, guidance, and strength close to us, we are prepared to fight in small and large battles.

CHALLENGE: Focus on becoming more aware and conscious of your negative thoughts today. We can fight courageously because we know the victory is already ours through Christ's sacrifice! Study Samuel 30 for more backstory on today's verse.

THOUGHTS:

DAY 11

FORGIVENESS OF OTHERS

Ephesians 4:31–32

Get rid of all bitterness, rage and anger, brawling and slander, along with every form of malice. Be kind and compassionate to one another, forgiving each other, just as in Christ God forgave you.

Forgiving those who wrong us is no walk in the park. One of the most incredible examples of radical forgiveness I've seen in my own life happened when I was in middle school. During an early morning service at my home church, a man walked in and opened fire on the pastor. At the time, our church did a lot of skits. When our pastor was shot, everyone thought it was all make believe. When we realized he was actually hurt, some of the guys in the audience tackled the gunman to the ground so he wouldn't shoot anyone else. The paramedics tried everything they could, but the pastor died an hour after he was shot. Our church mourned for years. Our pastor's wife and their kids had a long road of healing ahead of them. But the thing that's stuck with me the most, even all these years later, is how his wife spoke during interviews with local media. She forgave the man for killing her husband the day after the incident happened and expressed love for him. I remember watching this in astonishment. How could she forgive him so quickly?

Her answer was Jesus. To me, that sounded like a very "churchy" answer, but she went on to describe that having Jesus in her heart gave her the power to forgive. God transformed her heart; instead of becoming bitter because of the loss of her husband's life, she chose forgiveness that allowed both the gunman and her family to move forward in freedom. While it would have been easy for her to blame God for this unspeakable tragedy, she knew he wanted more for her and the others around her. He had something to give even amidst loss and sorrow.

If God can do that in her life, what makes us think he can't transform our lives too? No matter the hurt, God's grace is more than enough. When we enter a close, personal relationship with our heavenly Father, there is no room for grudges. Holding what someone did against them is creating less room for Jesus to be present in our lives. Without God's influence in our lives, we might not be able to ever forgive those who hurt us. With him, we have no excuse not to.

TAKEAWAY: Believing God has completely forgiven us and those around us when we ask him to come into our lives is hard to do. Our relationship with him gives us the ability to forgive those who wrong us.

CHALLENGE: Today, spend some time writing out all the people/things in your life that need your forgiveness. Jesus has already forgiven them. Ask him to change your heart so you can forgive them too.

THOUGHTS:

DAY 12

WHY JUDGING OTHERS ISN'T OUR JOB

James 4:12

There is only one Lawgiver and Judge, the one who is able to save and destroy. But you—who are you to judge your neighbor?

When Jesus came and taught others about his Father, his purpose was to save them, not judge them. Jesus knew the role of judge was his Father's and that *he* would hold people accountable at the right time. Jesus freely forgave those who earnestly desired it. I know I have sinned against God way more than anyone has ever sinned against me, so this drives me to step back from judging others. God is the one who truly knows the hearts of those around us and knows our hearts as well! In fact, I am thankful it's not my job to judge others around me. How exhausting that would be!

So how do we go about loving those around us when it is tempting to judge them? By aligning our hearts with God's purpose for us. We don't have the power to save others, but we do have the power of Christ living inside us! He desires all to come to him. When we open our hearts, his love reaches through our lives to bless those around us. And when it comes to loving those in our lives, Christ desires all to come to him. Loving these people includes speaking truth and forgiving those who wrong us. There is a major difference between lovingly letting your friend know they are not living up to their potential in Christ and just saying rude things that will tear down instead of build up.

We don't know the people around us from the inside out like our creator does. If those around us aren't living in line with the Word, we can gently share our concerns in love. However, we also must go into these conversations with humility, understanding that how things may look on the outside often doesn't reflect a person's inner reality. We are in this life together. It is the kindness of God that draws others to him and changes lives from the inside out, so let's make sure our life flows with kindness, not judgment.

TAKEAWAY: We are better together when we build one another up and encourage each other to fight against sin and hard circumstances. If we love others with a radical love, despite their sins, and show them a more fulfilling way to live in Christ, they will be more likely to change.

CHALLENGE: If there are people in your life that you need to make things right with, what is stopping you? Meditate on James 4:12 today. Remind yourself that you are also flawed and your encouragement to others can go far.

THOUGHTS:

WHEN THE PATH SEEMS UNCLEAR

Psalm 25:8–10

> *Good and upright is the L*ORD*; therefore he instructs sinners in his ways. He guides the humble in what is right and teaches them his way. All the ways of the L*ORD *are loving and faithful toward those who keep the demands of his covenant.*

've asked God, "What do you want me to do in this season?" or "Where do you want me to go?" far more than I can count. There's nothing wrong with these questions, and typically our intentions when asking these questions are pure. However, when these mini prayers become our only communication with God, we miss out on the fullness that he offers. God is our provider, and he does want to reveal his specific path for us, but he is so much more.

It's important to keep in mind that God is going to guide us in the small and mundane things even when we only ask him to move in big ways. And while God does sometimes answer our directional questions in huge reveals, often the little actions and everyday moments are when he reveals his truth. With these small events, he motions us to get closer to where he is and to come into the bounty and grace of the present moment. We don't need to know the path before he guides us on it. If we did, we would spend our time trying to get ahead of God, to push fast-forward in our journey.

I'm not sure if you've been there, but I know at some point all of us will face questions that we desperately want answered. Rest in knowing that not only do we follow a God who knows those answers, he knows us so intimately that he chooses to reveal more of himself to us in our questioning.

When the Lord seems silent in giving direction, keep visiting his Word, and remember the last thing he told you. Don't get discouraged if you feel like he is silent; he may just be asking you to draw closer to him. Cling to his Word and hold fast to his promises. In the decisions you make, ask the Lord to grant you peace about moving forward with his direction.

TAKEAWAY: We will never know all the answers to the questions we have for God about the future, and it's important in times of uncertainty to have faith. Because he knows what's best for us, we can walk with trust on the path the Lord clears for us with full confidence that it will bring life to us and others.

CHALLENGE: When we don't know where to go, we look for direction. I encourage you to read the rest of Psalm 25 and take notes. David asks for protection and guidance in this psalm, in a moment of desperation and uncertainty. I pray this passage comforts you as it does me.

THOUGHTS:

WORKING FOR GOD AND NOT FOR MAN

Colossians 3:23–24

Whatever you do, work at it with all your heart, as working for the Lord, not for human masters, since you know that you will receive an inheritance from the Lord as a reward. It is the Lord Christ you are serving.

t can be discouraging to work hard without recognition from others. It's important to know that God always sees your heart and your work. Imagine a world where everyone is doing the best they can at what they love and giving the glory to God. That sounds like heaven to me. Rick Warren says it best: "Work becomes worship when you dedicate it to God and perform it with an awareness of his presence."[1]

All the work we do can become heavenly gain if there is an intention to honor him. Even if we are not appreciated by the world for the work we do, Christ intimately sees our intentions. He knows the battle we fight in our day-to-day lives. Our job title does not define our worth, but if we pay more attention to our paychecks, coworkers' opinions, or the circle of people around us than to Christ's love and desire for our souls, we can get caught finding our worth in worldly things. If the only approval we seek is Christ's, we won't get distracted by other, less-accurate measures of our accomplishments or feel down when we don't get the recognition we think we deserve from others.

There is a place for you and me at the table of God, and

---

1   Rick Warren, *The Purpose Driven Life* (Grand Rapids, MI: Zondervan, 2002), page 67.

there are no work requirements. Whether we're in school or have an employer, if we work from the overflow of the love we receive from God, we will never be victims of comparison, anger, or burnout. The position of our hearts in our work is crucial to how we perform. Are you in it for yourself? Recognition from others? Joy is waiting for you on the other side of humility in your everyday life.

TAKEAWAY: There are periods in our lives where what we do might change, but our purpose does not. In these transitional times, try to find all the places you can shine the light you have to others. If effort is made in the services we are performing, every good line of work gives glory to God.

CHALLENGE: I challenge you to write the following on a sticky note or as a reminder in your phone to prompt yourself to recall who your real boss is: "Everything I do today can honor the Lord. I work for God, not for myself and not for people." Writing "not for man" reminds us that we are not slaves to men on earth, and instead our work is for the Lord. Put this reminder in a place where you will see it every day. May this inspire you to live in kindness, put more effort into what you do, and see your work from a heavenly perspective.

THOUGHTS:

DAY 15

WISDOM

Proverbs 3:7–8

Do not be wise in your own eyes; fear the LORD and shun evil. This will bring health to your body and nourishment to your bones.

The word *proverb* comes from a Hebrew word that means "to rule or to govern." When we read the book of Proverbs, we do so knowing it imparts advice for governing our lives. In a world that doesn't focus on how to live a holy life, holding Proverbs close to your heart is a wise decision.

There are a lot of truths out in the world we can choose to believe or not. But most aren't the whole truth, just a major (or minor) twist of the real thing. Take the news, for example. A lot of stories we are told, or footage we are shown, are edited to portray a certain message that might not have a respect for the entire story. When discerning the facts in these stories, or making decisions in our lives, wisdom gives us the opportunity to test the claims our world offers us. Gaining true wisdom begins with what Proverbs 3:7–8 prompts us to do. Becoming a "wiser" person starts with fearing the Lord and shutting out the enemy's schemes.

If you read today's verses, you'll see the strongest people hold godly wisdom tightly. Want to prosper in all you do? Seek out wisdom and turn every aspect of your life over to God, who has a plan for each of our lives. Finances, love life, friendships, family, work, you name it—he has a holy way to pursue these things.

Those who don't embrace the teaching and instruction

God's truth and wisdom offers live their lives as if drinking from a polluted stream. While the water will quench your thirst in the short term, it will make you sick if you keep drinking it. Those who seek God's wisdom find the truth about how the world works and how they should live. They drink from a pure stream, because inviting truth into your life lets God give you wisdom. This water offers life because its source is clean.

We've all drunk from a dirty stream at some point in our lives, but the key is to stop once we realize it's polluted, instead of ignoring the truth and continuing in our selfish ways. When we make the decision to pursue wisdom, all the litter and other pollutants slowly filter out of our stream, leaving only clean, crisp running water behind. All it takes to make the transition from murky to clean water is allowing the Word to become your litmus test, your standard, for distinguishing wise decisions from foolish ones.

TAKEAWAY: Wisdom must be pursued and practiced. To grow in it, you must work on strengthening it, just like any muscle. Are you pursuing wisdom?

CHALLENGE: I challenge you to read a chapter of Proverbs a day. There are only thirty-one chapters, so you can get through the entire book in a single month! Soak in its wisdom daily.

THOUGHTS:

MAKE MOVES, NOT EXCUSES

Romans 8:5–6

Those who live according to the flesh have their minds set on what the flesh desires; but those who live in accordance with the Spirit have their minds set on what the Spirit desires. The mind governed by the flesh is death, but the mind governed by the Spirit is life and peace.

Our sinful nature and the Spirit of God are in direct opposition to one another. We often become aware of our sin because we feel the tension between wanting to do what the Spirit encourages us to do and the instant gratification the flesh desires. As we become more aware of the dangerous effects of all we think, see, and hear, we develop a stronger desire to change our old patterns. The Bible says that the heart of man is wicked and sinful, but we weren't born to live in sin. So how do we combat sin?

For us to flourish in life, we must first get rid of the filth. I'm not sure what your sin or struggle is, but I know for some of you it feels crippling to live in it. You want to do what's right, but another voice enters in at the last second and makes you compromise. It feels like a vicious cycle, and that's because it is.

We must start being serious about who and what we surround ourselves with. The music we listen to, the people we follow, and images we choose to look at all make a difference. We soak in information all day, and the new data we take in creates thoughts. If we are consuming unhealthy ideas—ideas that are harmful to our heart, mind, and soul—every day, how can we expect any positive results in our fight against the enemy? There are times when we cannot change the environment in which we dwell, but we can control what we read, watch, and listen to. Sin starts in the heart, travels to the mind, and ends in action.

Jesus is our saving grace. He is more powerful than ANY sin. In fact, he already died to wash away anything you're struggling with. Your toughest struggle can become lighter while walking with Jesus if you hold his Word close and invite him into your heart/situation every day. Jesus is not afraid of your sin or disgusted with who you are, because you are not defined by your sin.

TAKEAWAY: Walking according to the Spirit provides a life of peace. The sins you're struggling with right now were already dealt with on the cross. You aren't bound to them anymore. Observe what you take in daily and get real with Jesus. Let him know you're frustrated and willing to change. He'll be there to guide you every step of the way. He wants you to walk in freedom.

CHALLENGE: Chew on Romans 8 for a while (it's deep, y'all). Pay attention to how the Lord instructs us to walk according to the Spirit. After you read it, write out a verse that you'd like to believe more for yourself. For me, it's Romans 8:12–13.

THOUGHTS:

DAY 17

SHAPE ME

Isaiah 64:8

Yet you, LORD, are our Father. We are the clay,
you are the potter; we are all the work of your
hand.

Watching a potter make the specific masterpiece they set out to create is an amazing process. The clay starts out as a big lump or block. As the potter spins the clay around on their wheel, it becomes shaped and molded to what the potter desires for that piece of clay.

Have you ever thought of your life as a piece of clay? The Father is shaping and molding you into the masterpiece he wants you to be. No two pieces of pottery are the same. There may be major similarities, but every piece is unique, complete with its own set of strengths and weaknesses. Like pottery, we weren't meant to all look, act, or be the same. Trusting the Father to make something incredible of your life is a process. It takes patience, trust, and daily devotion.

We may not realize how much we are changing and growing day by day. Think back to the person you were five years ago. Slightly different? Totally different? Even if there is a slight change in who you are now versus then, what's to say you won't grow to be more confident, loving, or forgiving in five more years from today? Growth does not happen overnight, but reading the incredible words God has written for us and about himself can change us in an instant. Imagine investing time every day to read, water the friendships you have, and get vulnerable with God and others. How life-changing would that be over time?

TAKEAWAY: God is our potter, and we are the clay. Our lives may look messy to us, but throughout this life we are continually being molded into masterpieces by the Lord. By looking outside of our present circumstances and pursuing Christ through life's ups and downs, we allow the Father to do his mighty work in us.

CHALLENGE: Isaiah 64 is a cry from the Lord's people who desperately want him to reveal himself despite their past sins. The Israelites had sinned by creating idols in their lives. You and I can probably resonate with that on some level, but they cried out for mercy and asked to be forgiven. They wanted deliverance from living for the selfish desires of themselves. They also realized how much they could be growing in the Lord and wanted a restart. Isaiah 64:8 is a verse I encourage you to memorize. Today, find a piece of paper or sticky note and write this verse on it. Place it in your car, on your mirror, or in your room, and read it any time you come across it.

THOUGHTS:

DAY 18

REMAIN IN LOVE

John 15:9–10

As the Father has loved me, so have I loved
you. Now remain in my love. If you keep my
commands, you will remain in my love, just as
I have kept my Father's commands and remain
in his love.

I n the gospel of John, John sees Jesus' amazing love in everything Jesus does because John spent a lot of time with him. He spent so much time with Jesus that he was one of the lucky guys able to document some of the many miracles and conversations Jesus had with others. Jesus' words in John 15:9–10 are a command to his followers to stay in God's love.

It is vital we stay close to Jesus so we know what he wants us to do. By keeping the Lord's commands, we remain in his love. Now, I'm not sure about you, but to me the word *commands* typically comes with a negative connotation. However, Scripture says that for believers it is a *delight* to follow the Lord. It is God's love for us and our love for him that makes obeying his commands a joy.

The world presents love as a word to throw around and take lightly, when love is much deeper than something we say to others. Love is an action, and it takes commitment. When we are acting in love, we listen and serve without expecting anything in return from those we are serving. We know we are honoring and loving God when we are living in alignment with John 15:10, keeping the ways of the Lord close and following in his path. Like John, we should be so committed to following Jesus that we spend time close to him, soaking up every word we can. When we focus on getting close to Jesus, his love surrounds us. I know my friends love me when they take time out of their schedules to hang out, ask questions, and are there for me during the hard times. God shows us friendship and love in all these ways and more! In fact, he loves us so much that he knows we live our best lives by following his commands (which is why he encourages us to do so!).

TAKEAWAY: God is always there, but it's easy to drift away if we are not actively seeking him. We are so loved, and we can remain in his love by holding close to him and to what he desires of us on earth.

CHALLENGE: You will encounter a few people today who are in desperate need of love. I encourage you to go out of your way for one you meet. This person might need someone to listen to them, your willing hands of service, or even a prayer. Ask the Lord to give you the right words to say and the courage to step up to love those around you.

THOUGHTS:

LOOKING TO THE FUTURE

James 4:13–15

Now listen, you who say, "Today or tomorrow we will go to this or that city, spend a year there, carry on business and make money." Why, you do not even know what will happen tomorrow. What is your life? You are a mist that appears for a little while and then vanishes. Instead, you ought to say, "If it is the Lord's will, we will live and do this or that."

One of the most uncertain words is *tomorrow*. But why? It seems so harmless, right? In my life, I've experienced friends passing away at a young age and the houses of people I know going up in flames. Those are tragic realities, but it could be anyone's reality. We just never know. I've come to terms with the fact that tomorrow may not look like what I think. In fact, tomorrow is not promised at all.

Planning our next steps by ourselves without God's intervention creates a selfish lifestyle. We begin living for ourselves and acting on our own narrow knowledge of the situation instead of aligning with God's big-picture plan. We end up walking paths not designed for us. This can happen when we get out of touch with God's voice by following distractions that end up leading us away from him. I used to think I wouldn't be affected by the things around me, even when I wasn't spending time with Jesus for weeks on end. But when we start making our own plans without listening to what God wants, our thoughts start to change to what the world wants from us.

When planning for the future, it's important to keep in mind that God's plans will prevail whether we listen to and try to follow him or if we don't. They might not always be what we expect—in fact, they *rarely* are—but we can be secure in the knowledge that God sees farther and plans better than we can.

TAKEAWAY: Tomorrow isn't promised, and we won't live forever on this earth. Remember the things of God are eternal. Setting your mind to a perspective that looks beyond you and your earthly desires—a life with Christ—will give you fuel to keep going in this life. I like to practice this mindset by making myself aware of the things that are eternal (like Christian friendships), and sometimes even writing them down. There is joy in following the will of God for our lives and remembering what truly matters!

CHALLENGE: If you are hesitant to boldly walk into something that is good and from God, get in the habit of telling yourself, "Tomorrow isn't promised," and do what God is calling you toward immediately after. If you have to, count down from five and go for it!

THOUGHTS:

LET GO OF SHAME

Genesis 3:9–10

But the LORD God called to the man, "Where are you?" He answered, "I heard you in the garden, and I was afraid because I was naked; so I hid."

sn't it crazy how the first feeling Adam and Eve expressed in the garden after they sinned was shame? I remember listening to a sermon on the topic of shame in our everyday lives. I suddenly understood why shame can so easily creep into our minds. Shame was never introduced until sin was.

The sin we often are guilty of committing is a mixture of failure and pride. Because of this, we must acknowledge when we sin, and confess and turn away. If we don't, shame can easily bare its ugly face, making us feel like we need to hide from God. There is a difference between shame and conviction as well. Conviction—knowing we need to repent and change—is healthy and of God. Sometimes God will give us an awareness of what we did wrong and nudge us in a direction that is honoring to him. Shame—wanting to run from ourselves and hide from God—is not of God, and the enemy will use it as a tool to drive a wedge in your relationship with Jesus. So, much like sin, we must combat shame when it tries to take hold in our lives!

If we're not careful, what Adam and Eve felt after eating the fruit in the garden can control a lot of our decisions. Before sin, the earth's first humans were "both naked, and they felt no shame" (Genesis 2:25). But after they sinned, shame was their reflex because their eyes were opened to their disobedience. Shame prompted them to hide from the only one who could help them.

When Adam answers the Lord after he is called out in the garden, he is afraid and aware of the sinful being he is. And Adam and Eve hid because they knew they had screwed up big time. Sin broke the unity that God and humans had at that time. But God's love is stronger than any sin or shame. This is a turning point in the creation story because God was heartbroken that Eve and Adam had chosen against him. But he knew he would make a way for humans to live in harmony with him again. The gap between God and humanity would be mended.

Thousands of years later, Jesus stepped on the scene to cross the great divide for you and me. He defeated shame through his sacrificial death, and now you and I can have confidence in the forgiveness he offers (more on that later).

TAKEAWAY: There is no reason to be afraid like Adam was in the garden. There is no sin that Jesus hasn't defeated. We can have confidence that there is no need to hide anymore. Walk out into the light so you can be guided by his truth.

CHALLENGE: Be present today in all the things you walk into. There is freedom in becoming aware of the Lord's work and his presence all around you. Walk in awareness today.

THOUGHTS:

TAKING RESPONSIBILITY FOR YOURSELF

Genesis 3:11–12

And he said, "Who told you that you were naked? Have you eaten from the tree that I commanded you not to eat from?" The man said, "The woman you put here with me—she gave me some fruit from the tree, and I ate it."

When we fall into sin, it's easy to blame someone else. Pushing sin onto someone other than ourselves and acting as if we are not at fault was one of the very first reactions humans had to sin.

Adam and Eve were no different than we are. They didn't have the technology or knowledge we have today, but they had a sin problem just like you and me. When God asked the two of them if they did exactly what he told them not to in the garden, Adam was so ashamed that he blamed it on Eve! (C'mon, man!) Yet even as they took a bite of fruit from the forbidden tree, they were aware of what they had done. After their fall into sin, the two of them were immediately ashamed of being naked in God's presence. Although they played different parts in this sinful act, they were both at fault.

Many times we will be tempted in life and cave in to those temptations, but God always promises forgiveness if we admit our failures to him. Prayer is vital to protecting ourselves from the schemes of the enemy. Jesus openly prayed, many times in front of his disciples and in public. The evil one doesn't have the power to block our prayers from reaching God, so pray with boldness! God is with us in our circumstances and wants us to make the best decisions that leave no room for shame, worry, or regret.

Transformation occurs when we take responsibility for our sinful nature and confess it to the one who can work in our hearts. Let's be honest when we've done wrong. I know I've struggled with mentally placing the blame on others. And although I usually do not admit it to them, I must confess to God that I need help to stay away from playing "the blame game." Blaming others instead of confessing sins causes resentment toward people you want to love better. Choose righteousness by asking the Lord to come into the situation(s) where you're tempted to place blame and then have a conversation with that person. Ask God to bring forward the thoughts that are harmful, so you can tackle them together.

TAKEAWAY: We may often be tempted to sin, but God has provided his Spirit to help us as we walk through life. So lean into the Spirit of God by inviting God into the "ugly" (or sinful) spots of your life. Although it is tempting to blame others when we mess up, God honors a heart that stands its ground in a fight against sin. It is so freeing when we admit to our mistakes and work through them.

CHALLENGE: Next time you're faced with a decision to blame others, ask yourself, "Does this lead me closer to God?" and then proceed if it does. If not, step away!

THOUGHTS:

REFLECTING HIM

2 Peter 1:3–4

His divine power has given us everything we need for a godly life through our knowledge of him who called us by his own glory and goodness. Through these he has given us his very great and precious promises, so that through them you may participate in the divine nature, having escaped the corruption in the world caused by evil desires.

When reading 2 Peter 1:3, I often feel a deep longing to reflect God in a way that both feels fulfilling to me and honors him. When I look around at our world—one that is corrupt in so many ways—I realize God is asking us to be bold in our faith and celebrate the uniqueness he has instilled inside each one of us.

If I were to ask you if you are being fulfilled by what you're currently pursuing in life, would you say yes? For most of my life, my answer was no. Without realizing it, I followed what I thought would fulfill me by watching the lives of others. I dated people I knew were not right for me, got into toxic friendships (and sometimes was a toxic friend myself), and spent way too much time and money buying things I didn't need. If I had been aware of the truth I was called by God to reflect his own glory and goodness, I would have strutted through life as the Chelsea that God made me to be, and not the Chelsea I *thought* everyone wanted to see.

We can live a life that not only reflects Christ but also brings immense joy and love to our hearts and to others. By seeking the life that is available to us through Jesus' sacrifice, we live out the promises found in the Word of God. That may sound intense and serious (and you could argue that it is) but the decisions you make now set the trajectory of the path you'll walk in the future. If you choose a job solely for the money, you won't live a fulfilled life; but if you choose a job you enjoy that fits your gifts and calling, you could live out of the love you have for what you do and the people you get to serve daily! The world will say that your fulfillment will come from being financially on top and having a picture-perfect lifestyle, but you'll be attempting to fill a void that only Christ can fill. We are all given unique desires and talents to reflect certain parts of our creator. How *beautiful*!

TAKEAWAY: Jesus has given us different people, resources, and blessings to help us live a godly life that reflects him. The desires the world offers are evil, but we can be set apart by walking in God's immense power. We are unique reflections of Christ.

CHALLENGE: Remembering what is promised in God's Word brings peace and joy. Since today's verse comes from 2 Peter, spend some time today highlighting the promises in the first chapter of Peter's second letter. Reflect on those promises once you're finished. Remember, the entire Bible is filled with God's promises! If you are currently studying the Bible in a group setting or on your own, you can apply this method anytime you are reading the Word.

THOUGHTS:

ACTIVELY WAIT ON THE LORD

Psalm 27:13–14

I remain confident of this: I will see the goodness of the LORD in the land of the living. Wait for the LORD; be strong and take heart and wait for the LORD.

Are you currently in a season of waiting? Have you been stuck asking God the same questions about the future?

You are not alone. Almost everyone is waiting for something, whether it be the person they'll spend the rest of their life with, a job offer, or simply a vacation break. Waiting can be frustrating. It can also come with confusion, a loss of focus, and bitterness toward others. It's a hard place to be in, and often we end up asking God, "Why?"

This place of confusion and frustration might leave you feeling alone and far from the Lord. Trust me, I've been in this place time and time again. It's hard to believe God is working on our behalf while we wait for days, months, or sometimes even years. We think God has given up on us when things don't go as planned. One of the most comforting things to know about the Lord is that he is always present during the waiting. If we dig deep into the Bible, we see that it shares real stories of women and men waiting on the Lord for long periods of time. It would be cool to say that most of them were faithful and patient (and some were), but a lot of them tried to take the situations into their own hands. Spoiler alert: Not really a smart move, but hey, we've all been there!

God made Moses and the Israelites wait in the desert for forty years before his promise was fulfilled, and they wouldn't even be the ones to experience the promised land (their children would be). But why did he make them wait? Because they disobeyed in the beginning! The Israelites were given an opportunity to fully rely on the Holy Spirit, but they decided to lean on their own understanding of their present circumstances. I think if I had to wait forty years for God's promises, I might give up early on, if I'm honest. Moses was one of the most patient and trusting men in the Bible. But at times, even Moses got frustrated, confused, and lonely. He doubted what the Lord told him to do at times and relied on himself. Despite that, the Lord was still faithful, and honored Moses's years of waiting by allowing him a glimpse of the promised land before he died. This serves as a reminder that the Bible is filled with stories of *real* people, trying their best to navigate real-life problems—alongside a God who looked to help them through those struggles.

Patience always comes before an answered prayer. But "waiting" doesn't mean we do nothing or become stagnant in our walk with the Lord. These periods of "waiting" are often the times where God helps us grow, and I'm amazed at the amount of personal and spiritual development I, and others, have experienced during these periods. In the end, you'll be thankful you had these experiences, so keep your current situation in perspective and pray that the Lord will allow you to have a patient heart!

TAKEAWAY: God knows waiting can be hard. If we trust that the Lord is there in the midst of our waiting, he will do more in our lives than we could ever imagine. His plan is always worth the wait.

CHALLENGE: When you feel alone, communicate with God in whatever way feels most natural to you. Write out your prayers, sing worship songs out loud, or create artwork. Tell him your concerns and ask him for a patient heart. Whether you hear him or not, he is always there in the waiting. Be quiet and listen for his still, small voice.

THOUGHTS:

DAY 24

INTENTIONALITY

1 John 3:18

Dear children, let us not love with words or speech but with actions and in truth.

n our society, people are quick to put themselves first for selfish reasons. We love our image, our reputation, and our wants. It's easy to chase shiny things, be in relationships that might boost your status, and live an "it's all about me" kind of life. But all those things last a short amount of time and attempt to fill a God-sized hole in our hearts.

As I read through a few of Bob Goff's books, I was taken back by the amazing biblical advice he imparts to his readers through the stories he tells. When reading *Everybody Always*, I was inspired to be more intentional about loving and being with others. I asked myself many questions after I was done reading and reflecting. How often am I physically present with people but not mentally or spiritually present? How often are my attempts at loving others driven by my pride or selfish ambitions?

If you take one look at the world we live in, it's easy to tell that we are self-centered and self-obsessed. We gauge our self-worth by the number of likes on our social media pages or the recognition of others on the internet. I've even been guilty of thinking people with bigger social media followings were more special to God than I am! We're more concerned about our status and what others think of us than what God thinks of us. It's a vicious cycle that doesn't end until we make a conscious decision to stop it.

So how do we live a selfless life? Become aware of the areas in which you are selfish, then get to the root of why you feel that way toward something or someone. Is it driven by fear? The need to be the best? Then find a way to break that selfish response. There is a difference between giving your best and doing your best for the sake of outshining others. This is a *tiny* example, but sometimes I'll sense myself becoming jealous of another girl, and I find myself upset that I started that thought pattern. So my response is to honestly compliment or encourage something I like about her to combat the negative thoughts that attempt to take over. When we practice truly loving others, it starts to become a more natural response in our daily lives. Humility is gained in the process of living a selfless life. God sees your heart, and he will reward the humble.

We are called to love our neighbors for their own good, not for selfish gain. Although it can be hard to tell between the two, ask yourself what your true motives are. Are you prioritizing someone else's needs in order to feel better or to look good to those around you? When was the last time you helped one of your friends without them knowing? When was the last time you helped a stranger without posting about it on social media? You may lose money, time, or something else when you extend a hand to someone in need, but you gain godly character, reward in heaven, and an increased awareness of the blessings you have.

TAKEAWAY: A selfless life is a good life. Feeding selfish desires enslaves you to earthly idols and drains the joy from life. Serving Jesus and his people is what we were created to do, and it leads to a full and fulfilled existence.

CHALLENGE: Show kindness and love today to someone you normally wouldn't. Do it without telling anyone about it. Maybe write a note to someone and pick up a drink or candy bar for them at the gas station. That's just one idea. Get creative! Experience the joy in simply loving others well.

THOUGHTS:

DAY 25

IMPORTANCE OF COMMUNITY

2 Corinthians 6:14–15

Do not be yoked together with unbelievers. For what do righteousness and wickedness have in common? Or what fellowship can light have with darkness? What harmony is there between Christ and Belial? Or what does a believer have in common with an unbeliever?

f the apostle Paul were alive today, the message I believe he might preach to us all is the gospel (of course), and also the importance of who your friends are. In his second letter to the Corinthians, Paul tried to emphasize the importance of community and surrounding yourself with like-minded Christians. He knew that if the church in Corinth continued surrounding themselves with idol worshipers, it wouldn't be very long before they were led down a path of destructive sin. Our interactions with others tend to reinforce certain behaviors, and those behaviors become habits over time. This is why having the right circles of influence is so crucial.

As Christians, we should look for people who are going to push us toward God and inspire us to live out the unique missions he's called each of us to follow. Oftentimes, it can seem incredibly unnatural to get involved in a diverse church community that includes believers we wouldn't naturally gravitate toward. But the friendships we form through relationship with Jesus are associations that will carry into eternity. These people can pray for you, hold you to your promise of righteous living, and encourage you in your walk. Your life can offer the same to others. Fellowship should be a big part of our lives; good relationships with others of faith also reinforce a close relationship with the Lord. Without a good group of people to continually encourage you, it's easy to step away from the path God created for you.

God often speaks of the importance of fellowship throughout his Word. If we surround ourselves with people who have opposite values, morals, or beliefs, it can be hard to stay true to our own. Oftentimes, we end up being someone we never wanted to be. If you want to have a healthy and virtuous life, look for people who desire to have Christ at the center of who they are.

TAKEAWAY: It's hard to pursue the will of God if you're not around people who want the same thing. If you want harmony in your friendships or romantic relationships, make sure the people you interact with are also seeking God in their daily lives.

CHALLENGE: Take a survey of the five closest relationships in your life. Do the friends you surround yourself with share your life values and morals? Are these people constantly encouraging you to improve your life, or are they leading you to do things you know aren't in line with who you want to be?

THOUGHTS:

DAY 26

JUST BREATHE

Matthew 11:29

Take my yoke upon you and learn from me, for I am gentle and humble in heart, and you will find rest for your souls.

'll be the first one to admit that, at times, my focus and attention are being pulled in a million different directions. I have schoolwork to finish, emails to send (Do they ever end?!), laundry to wash, friends to keep in touch with, and a room to clean. Then I go to sleep, wake up, and do it all over again. It's easy to get buried in my "to-do's" and forget about taking care of myself.

It's important to be responsible and meet your obligations, but recently one of my friends reminded me that if I decide to focus on everything, I'm putting my energy and effort into nothing. Meaning, we can't focus on the important things/people in our lives if we're saying yes to everything, because we're then saying no to what matters most (relationships, time with Jesus, etc.). I was letting my life control me, and I wasn't taking proper care of myself. My friends could see that I was letting my work life (filming videos, recording podcasts, traveling) get in the way of my health because I thought I needed to do it all.

If you keep living life with the pedal to the metal, trying to squeeze every drop out of each day, you will drain your "cup" and have nothing left to give. You aren't doing anyone, or yourself, any good if your cup is drained.

I think humans tend to put our to-do's before taking

proper care of ourselves. We give ourselves to the people we love wholeheartedly, and sometimes that can be draining. Typically, the times when I show myself the most care are when I am sick and forced to do so. Physically and mentally draining yourself just sets you back farther from your goals. It becomes a constant cycle of regain and drain. When we are stressed out, self-care is one of the first things we put on the back burner.

I know it is hard to give yourself time and space when you have so many other things that you could be doing, but remember it is harder to be of service to others if you are not taking care of yourself. So try to regularly take some time for yourself, and find your rest in Jesus. "Treating yourself" doesn't always mean a pedicure and spending money on shopping (there's a time and place for that); truly treating yourself involves nourishing your mind, body, and soul. Go outside and take a nature walk, take a nap with your pup (or cat), or make a healthy meal for yourself that you take time to create. Your body will thank you!

TAKEAWAY: There are many times in the Bible where Jesus tells us rest and to rest in him. A big part of rest is nourishing your heart, mind, body, and soul. What actions do you need to take today to rest well? Remember, you can't pour from an empty cup. Take care of yourself, because you are worth it!

CHALLENGE: Take a few minutes out of your day to do some good for yourself. Go on a leisurely walk. Watch an episode of your favorite show. Buy yourself a ridiculously overpriced coffee. Put on your favorite outfit (which may just be your pajamas)! Meditate on your favorite Bible verse. Go to sleep early and get at least eight hours of rest. God wants us to be physically healthy so we can serve others and maintain our spiritual fitness as well.

THOUGHTS:

DAY 27

WALK THROUGH THE OPEN DOOR

Psalm 25:4–5, 9

Show me your ways, LORD, teach me your paths.
Guide me in your truth and teach me, for you
are God my Savior, and my hope is in you all
day long. [. . .] He guides the humble in what is
right and teaches them his way.

Have you ever wanted something so badly that when it fails to happen, you feel defeated and alone?

In high school, I would often fall head over heels for a boy, just to find out he had no interest in me. I would get excited about possible work opportunities, only to find out they'd already contacted someone else for the job.

Life's not always easy when the open door you'd hoped for ends up closing with little to no explanation. There's a concept I heard a long time ago that didn't made sense to me until recently: If it doesn't open, it's not your door. God always directs you down the path he's predestined for you, so if it doesn't work out, it's his way of saying, "That's not where you're meant to go." I often found myself getting frustrated at God when things didn't turn out the way I hoped. I would want something so badly only to watch it disappear right in front of me. I encourage you to pray for guidance and knowledge. Pray for God's plan to be revealed to you amidst the confusion and uncertainty. God wants us to call out to him, not lean on our own understanding.

I'm a firm believer that everything in life happens for a reason. If God closes a door in your life, realize he has a reason for it and walk away in obedience to the Lord. Don't try to force something that isn't meant to be.

If you want something so badly you can't stand it, ask for it. All God wants from us is to look to him in our choices, and in our everyday lives. How can something we want be given to us if we don't even seek our God to begin with? If we seek Christ with all our heart, he will deliver the best path. And if he doesn't give us the answer we hope for, it's always for a reason. The door will either open with blessing from the Lord, or it wasn't meant for you in the first place.

TAKEAWAY: Take notice of the doors God closes along your life's journey, and the ones he leaves open. Trust God and trust his plan. You will not regret it.

CHALLENGE: I encourage you to write out all your concerns to the Lord and pray over them out loud. Continue to update your list or letter as time goes on. The answer will always be "yes," "no," or "wait."

THOUGHTS:

YOU ARE UNIQUELY YOU

Genesis 30:1

When Rachel saw that she was not bearing Jacob any children, she became jealous of her sister. So she said to Jacob, "Give me children, or I'll die!"

omparison and envy are common emotions, and jealousy can get the best of us if we're not careful to stop it in its tracks. A good example of jealousy run riot is the story of Leah and Rachel. Rachel was so upset that her sister, Leah, was having baby after baby while she was unable to conceive, she literally wanted to *die*.

Comparison robs us of joy. These days, being content with what we have and how we look is a struggle. If you ask a group of women what one of their biggest challenges is, the overwhelming answer will be comparing themselves to others. I've had to take breaks from social media platforms because I get caught up comparing my highs and lows to the amazingly photographed, precisely videoed, fabulous lives of others. We need to learn how to be content; a life without contentment puts the focus on ourselves and not who we were designed to glorify.

Accept your uniqueness: Think of something you are good at, and then think how long you have been practicing that skill. Maybe it's running, cooking, or making art. God designed us to be one of a kind. Life would be so boring if we all looked alike, dressed alike, and had the same talents and skills. You have likely worked to develop the unique gifts God gave you. Celebrate them, and instead of envying a friend for her gift, celebrate her. Be happy for the strengths of others. Whether it is the physical attributes of others, their mental capabilities, or their material possessions, we can either make ourselves feel better or worse about ourselves based on our evaluations. Every day, make a conscious effort to see yourself as God sees you—which, I'll admit, can be a struggle! Remember that comparison is a selfish game. See the real person behind the external attributes. Consider a person's feelings, and work hard to compliment others from the heart. You never know—they could also be struggling with a comparison battle.

TAKEAWAY: Kick worldly expectations to the curb. Not only does comparison steal our joy, it steals our contentment and our desire to live a godly life. When we compare ourselves with others, we are not using an accurate measuring stick. Dragging around the world's expectations keeps us from fully experiencing what God has in store. We cheat ourselves out of God's blessings when we try to live the life we see others living. When you live your own life and stop envying someone else's, you see your blessings more clearly.

CHALLENGE: Let's rejoice in our strengths, work on our weaknesses, and celebrate each other for the unique people we are. Today, look for five people to give genuine compliments to. At the end of the day, I write down how it went so you can be encouraged to live another day like this one.

THOUGHTS:

DEAR TO HIS HEART

1 John 3:1–2

See what great love the Father has lavished on us, that we should be called children of God! And that is what we are! The reason the world does not know us is that it did not know him. Dear friends, now we are children of God, and what we will be has not yet been made known. But we know that when Christ appears, we shall be like him, for we shall see him as he is.

f I were to ask you what makes you uniquely you, what would you say? Maybe you're incredibly talented at sports, great at your job, or gifted at different forms of art. It's easy to define ourselves by what we do instead of who we are.

If I'm not careful, my head can often become filled with doubts. Am I good enough? Am I smart enough? It can become easy to get caught up in what I and others think about myself and forget about what the creator of the universe thinks about me.

When I was flipping through the pages of my Bible recently, a certain word stuck out to me: beloved. I don't think it was an accident I came across this word when I was struggling with how much I define myself by the things I do on this earth. *Beloved* is defined in the dictionary as "greatly loved; dear to the heart." Its synonyms are *cherished, precious, sweet, darling.* When we think of God calling us beloved or his beloved, he is also calling us cherished, precious, and dear to him. The beautiful thing about this is that in the Bible, the word *beloved* is almost always used when addressing God's children. It gives me so much comfort knowing that I am called beloved by the God who made the planets and sent his one and only Son to save the sins of his people. No matter what else I might do, my identity is beloved of God first and foremost!

TAKEAWAY: We need to stop thinking of ourselves as the star athlete or the class valedictorian. Although these achievements are great to celebrate, we need to remember who we are at the end of the day. We are solely God's children, and he calls us his own. He calls us his *beloved*, his darling, his precious, his cherished. Believing this truth helps us overcome feelings of unworthiness and gives us purpose in a broken world.

CHALLENGE: Next time doubts and insecurities pop up in your mind, remember who you are before you are tempted to define yourself by what you do. Today, spend some time writing out ten things Christ calls you and refer back to this list whenever you're doubting your place as a daughter/son of the King.

THOUGHTS:

DAY 30

HE IS NEAR

Psalm 145:18

The LORD is near to all who call on him, to all who call on him in truth.

Too many people see God as a distant voice or merely someone they hear about in church every Sunday. To some, he's a genie in a bottle who is only talked to if they have a need or deep pain.

There are so many different verses in the Bible that give us deep insight on who God really is. From these, we know he is loving, patient, merciful, forgiving, and all-knowing.

It's no mistake that the Bible frequently describes God as our Father. Matthew 23:9 says, "... for you have one Father, and he is in heaven." He cares for us endlessly and is the perfect example of how a father should be. So how can we get closer to God, our Father in heaven? All it takes is open communication. When you have exciting news, sudden problems, or an urgent need, talk to him in prayer. If you ever question if he wants to hear from you, be encouraged that he's always there and delights in his relationship with you. If we truly know him as our provider, creator, and Father, then we should want to be close to him and make every effort to do so.

You don't get closer to someone by just interacting with them when it's convenient for you or solely when you feel like it. Every good relationship requires a conscious effort to communicate and make time for each other. Picture your relationship with one of your best friends. Do you talk to them every day or only when you need something? Do you make an effort to learn more about their life and spend time with them, or just use them as a sounding board for your problems? The best relationships consist of two people giving to one another unconditionally. We can be confident that the Lord wants to spend time with us, so we need to have the same attitude and take the time to get to know him, through Bible study and prayer, in return.

When we stand at the gates of heaven, we want to embrace God and thank him for the relationship he so graciously gave us the opportunity to have. He already knows us better than we know ourselves, so getting to know him through relationship is a great joy and safe haven to us in this big world.

TAKEAWAY: God isn't a big, scary, faraway voice. He wants to be there for you. If we seek him, he will draw near. People try to make a relationship with God so complicated, but it's as simple as taking the time to build a relationship with him!

CHALLENGE: Take five minutes to talk to God. It's an easy but important beginning to drawing even closer to him! You can even write out your thoughts if you prefer.

THOUGHTS:

DAY 31

I'M DREAMIN'

Ephesians 3:20–21

Now to him who is able to do immeasurably more than all we ask or imagine, according to his power that is at work within us, to him be glory in the church and in Christ Jesus throughout all generations, for ever and ever! Amen.

When you picture your future, what do you see? What kind of person are you? What are you doing? Where do you live? We all have treasured dreams of an amazing someday. Though it's easy to let those dreams slip away when you hear discouragement—or even disapproval—from others. But if that dream is rooted deep inside of you, bringing it to God and submitting it to him is exciting. He will either provide the way and/or resources, or he'll let you know that there is something better in store.

When Paul was writing to the church at Ephesus, there was a strong need for the church to remember who God was and what he could do if they were all-in with his mission. We still need this reminder today! He can do much with even the little things we dedicate to him. As Matthew 17:20 says, it is important to know that even with the smallest amount of faith, dreams can be born into reality. Including yours.

Most of the world may encourage you to take leaps of faith or shots in the dark and not even ask what the Lord wants you to do with those dreams, but the Word of God says to take steps in faith. Which means: take steps in faith with him! Ask him what he has to say, where he would like to see you move, and he will always be with you. God can do immeasurably more with your steps taken in dedication to him than a stride taken all by yourself.

TAKEAWAY: Your prayers, dreams, and desires can become incredible stories you never thought possible when God enters the picture. How might God use your dreams right now?

CHALLENGE: Today, write out your answers to these three questions:

1. WHAT are you passionate about?
2. WHOM do you want to help during your time on earth?
3. What NEED do you see in the world?

Ask God to grow your desires and teach you the purpose behind the things you're doing. Even if you may not be where you want to be right now, remember the Lord is always faithful and always working things for your greatest good. He can do so much more when we entrust our paths to him than we can ever do by ourselves.

THOUGHTS:

DAY 32

MAKING
MISTAKES

Hebrews 4:16

*Let us then approach God's throne of grace with
confidence, so that we may receive mercy and
find grace to help us in our time of need.*

constantly tell myself I am not defined by my past mistakes. I am susceptible to believe I am defined by the partying I did in high school, the "bad boys" I dated that kept me from fully engaging in my spiritual life, or the unkind ways I've treated my friends. We can get stuck in this dangerous trap if we don't stop the lie that makes us believe we are defined by our past decisions.

Our culture often makes us believe we are only the sum of all the things we've done: our performance in school or at work, the success or failure of our relationships, the accumulation of material items or monetary wealth. Because our society has bought into this lie so deeply, it's no wonder that we often find ourselves becoming frustrated or despondent when we make a mistake or struggle with sin.

Mistakes can be hard to move past, but with God, it is possible. During my senior year of high school, I attended a Lecrae concert. He said something in between songs that has stuck with me since. He shouted: "There is grace today for yesterday's mistakes. Do you believe that?!" I remember getting so hyped in that moment, but I didn't understand the weight of the statement until I found friends who deeply cared about me. These are not superficial friendships that just looked good on the outside. Some conversations we've had were messy. These people encourage me despite my human flaws, despite the ways I've failed them or been unkind to them. These friends have shown me what it means to love someone and give them grace every day, like Jesus does for us.

Often, I am my biggest critic. Even after others have forgiven me, I can beat myself up for making mistakes or acting in a way that doesn't align with the way Christ would want us to behave. I need to believe what Lecrae shouted that night every single day. It is inevitable that I will make mistakes, so it is important I get familiar with what true grace is through Jesus.

After we make a mistake, we need to remember that God's throne is not intimidating. His presence is welcoming. Once we realize God has forgiven us, it's easier to forgive ourselves. No matter what mistake we make, he can change us from the inside out if we give him the space to do so in our hearts. We can boldly walk to him, because he intimately knows and understands our pain and struggle. And because he already paid the price for every mistake or error in judgment we have or ever will make, we can live our lives in confidence, extending grace to both ourselves and others.

TAKEAWAY: If you're having a hard time believing you are forgiven, this is your reminder. You can start fresh now and ask for help from your heavenly Father every step of the way.

CHALLENGE: Write out what you need to forgive yourself for and/or know you are forgiven for. Once you have written it out, ask the Lord to guide you in your journey of forgiveness. Remember that his grace is sufficient, even when your emotions tell you it isn't.

THOUGHTS:

DAY 33

MENTORS

1 Timothy 4:11–13

Command and teach these things. Don't let anyone look down on you because you are young, but set an example for the believers in speech, in conduct, in love, in faith and in purity. Until I come, devote yourself to the public reading of Scripture, to preaching and to teaching.

When I was growing up, I was encouraged to seek a mentor in my church. But every time I heard the word *mentor*, I envisioned an old lady with white hair sitting in a rocking chair (who, in my mind, resembled my adorable next-door neighbor). I never *really* knew what that type of relationship looked like until I became friends with a few women who were just a few steps ahead in life. Mentorship isn't as complicated as we make it out to be. My favorite thing about having the mentors I do is that we hang out in their homes and I get to see how they live with their families. It doesn't feel like an interview every time we meet, but rather that there is accountability for the way we all live our lives and make decisions.

We are not meant to walk through life alone, and it is of vital importance that we have wise and seasoned people to help us walk through the situations we have no idea how to navigate. A mentor is defined as "a trusted guide or counselor." A good mentor is usually a step or two ahead of you in life, is honest, and holds you accountable.

In the book of Timothy, Paul encourages Timothy to live a life of daily renewal of the mind and instructs him how to lead in his community. In 1 Timothy 4:11–13, we only see a sliver of the relationship these two guys had with each other.

Paul looked out for Timothy by encouraging him to live a life of accountability and instructing him to lead those around him by living purely in all areas. God wants us to have vibrant, inspiring, empowering relationships like these too!

TAKEAWAY: We all have roles in life that we were born into, but what about the roles we can *choose* to walk into? According to Titus 2:3–5, mentorship is a call on all of us. We get to grow with others! We need each other to flourish in life.

CHALLENGE: Do you have a mentor? Do you know someone you can mentor yourself? Pray for a mentor in your life and ask for that relationship to be established. Once you've identified someone who can be your mentor or who you can mentor (or both), arrange to meet in person, and meet often!

THOUGHTS:

GOD IS AT WORK

Zephaniah 3:17

The LORD your God is with you, the Mighty Warrior who saves. He will take great delight in you; in his love he will no longer rebuke you, but will rejoice over you with singing.

I once passed a church sign that read, "Can you see his miracles?" At first, I chuckled. It was such a bold statement, yet I couldn't help but ponder on all the times in life where I haven't clearly seen how God is at work. Sometimes there seems to be so much sin and suffering around us, God seems absent. When we get distracted by all the evil in the world, it can be hard to see that God's fingerprints are all over our lives.

In Zephaniah 3:17, God's joy echoes his people's. God is overjoyed because his people are full of joy because of him. God is overjoyed when we accept how much he loves us. This verse tells us that the Lord *sings* over us when we delight in him. How amazing!

When you see groups of people uniting for the cause of Christ and to share his name, God is at work. When you have a stirring to know more of who God is, he is at work. When justice is served in a terrible court case, God is at work. Even in the times where God seems to be gone because hurtful and evil things are happening, God has a purpose and he is working behind the scenes. As humans, we will never fully understand why God does what he does. But we can take comfort in his ultimate plan for all of creation, knowing that our perspective is limited compared to his.

The next time I pass the "Can you see his miracles?" sign, I'll be thankful that even when I feel blind to all that God is doing in the present, I can be reassured by his faithfulness and goodness in the past and know he is always working, no matter what I see right now. His payment for my sin continually tells me in my struggles and circumstances, "It's okay, it is finished, and I'll keep fighting for you." God is with us. He delights in us, and we should delight in his works daily.

TAKEAWAY: When you may not even realize it, God is working behind the scenes for you. God desires for us to have an awareness of who he is and what he is doing so that we can be confident in who we are through him.

CHALLENGE: I encourage you to record how you see God moving and where you'd like to see him move. Write down one thing the Lord has changed for your good over the past year and reflect.

THOUGHTS:

DAY 35

SEEKING HIM WHEN YOU CAN'T HEAR HIS VOICE

Psalm 34:10b

Those who seek the LORD lack no good thing.

Silence may not be a bad thing, but when you feel as if the Lord is silent in your life, it can be confusing. I've felt this more times than I can count, but as I've grown older I've come to know that he is there even when I cannot "hear" him.

There are a few things to remember when you cannot seem to hear God's voice. First, he wants nothing more than to speak to us and have a relationship with us. He wants our attention and our hearts. If you don't think the Lord wants to speak to you at all, it is unlikely you're attuned to his still, small voice.

Second, God speaks in many ways. Becoming attuned to his voice and able to recognize it in the different ways he speaks is a process, but it is encouraging to know that he does speak to us, if we are present enough to pay attention. You may be in the middle of making a decision and aren't sure what the Lord is telling you to do. If that is the case, know he is always speaking through his Word, through his people, and sometimes through signs and divine encounters.

Sometimes the Lord is silent because he is giving you a choice. The best thing to do in those situations is test your options to see if they're in line with the Word and pray that the Lord directs your mind and the desires of your heart to align with his. Remember, the intentions behind your choice are often more important than the choice. God sees the desires of our heart and sometimes looks after us by choosing to be still.

In the end, he is God, and we are his creation, so we may not understand why he does what he does, but we can trust that his divine plan exceeds this earth and the limits of our human minds. He is working everything together for his glory and our good even if we cannot immediately see that at times.

TAKEAWAY: We all have periods in our lives that make us question if God is there or if he's working in our lives, but no matter what we feel, he's there. Those who seek the Lord lack no good thing.

CHALLENGE: What was the last thing God told you? What was the last scripture you dwelt on? Go back to it. Remember the promise, and rest. He is faithful, even when you cannot see or hear him.

THOUGHTS:

ALLOWING GOD TO GUIDE YOUR PASSIONS

Proverbs 19:21

Many are the plans in a person's heart, but it is the LORD's purpose that prevails.

What's your answer when someone asks what you want to do for the rest of your life? I have yet to give a solid response to that question.

While I haven't yet identified my career path, God has placed certain things on my heart that I know get me fired up. I'm incredibly passionate about building community, loving others well, and seeing others grow. Above our passions, it is important we walk each day in faithfulness with God. If we submit our desires and longings to him, he will show us the way we should go in his time as well.

I recently spoke to a friend of mine about the mindset of the working world. He is a poet, writer, leader, and more. He is currently pushing himself to try different projects and not conform to the world's standard of success. He prayed over the decision for some time, then moved forward. I give him credit for paving his own path and following something God has clearly placed on his heart to do.

To identify your passion(s), it is important to be aware of the issues God has placed on your heart that you can help change, the groups of people you're enthusiastic about and can join, the creative ideas you find intriguing, where your God-given talents lie, and what makes you excited in life. What makes you angry, joyful, energized, or emotional?

To help identify where God is calling you to serve, consider your unique gifts and talents that may better the world.

Personally, I get fired up about the condition of the world and how much we individually need Jesus. When I hear about rape cases, I get angry. When I see an old married couple together having fun, my heart is full. A deep book that makes me think in a way I haven't before inspires me to share my thoughts by writing to others.

When added to my personal talents, my passions move me to pursue the next project the Lord lays on my heart. God has called you, and he is completely able to reveal your purpose to you, as long as you seek him.

TAKEAWAY: Remember that your purpose is not just about you—it's about what God wants to do through you. Your gifts and your passions exist to help serve others and bring joy!

CHALLENGE: If you feel stuck or don't know what you're passionate about/what to do with your passions, write out your frustration in a journal and pray over it. God wants us to discover our individual purpose more than we do ourselves. Pray for your true desires to be made known to you, and once you understand a little bit more about yourself and your desires/passions, write them down too.

THOUGHTS:

DAY 37

WISE LEADERSHIP

Proverbs 11:14

For lack of guidance a nation falls, but victory is won through many advisers.

Wat if I told you that you can be a leader and not be in charge? There are countless leaders in the Bible, but not all of them were in charge. In fact, those who *were* in charge were often influenced by their closest circle of friends. We are all leaders in some way.

I've gotten a lot of leadership guidance from Proverbs (like today's verse). King Solomon's wisdom is golden, and he is known to be one of the wisest people in history. True leaders strive for wisdom, and they seek guidance from someone who has done what they aspire to do or be.

In today's verse, Solomon talks about leadership of a nation. The main message from this verse is that we need people to hold us accountable to our position. This may look like meeting up once a week with a friend who knows our strengths and weaknesses. Someone who is willing to ask us hard questions and hold us to walking wisely. Are we using our power and responsibility well? Without a community of people to encourage each other and look at all the pros and cons of an issue, we would only see our side of the picture. But with wise guidance, prosperity is the medal awarded.

To be a leader in your life, you *must* live a life worthy of that calling. Walking with others in community is a big part of being a leader. You didn't end up in a leadership position by chance—those you're leading trust you! And they want to support you as well. The best leaders of the world have people around them speaking truth even when it may not be pleasant to hear. Do you have this in the relationships around you? People to call up when life goes awry? In the roles that you fill in your life, pay attention to those around you. Those relationships can help you and the people you're leading flourish.

TAKEAWAY: Impactful leaders surround themselves with people who encourage, speak honestly, and are not afraid to let others know when they are off track. Individuals in these support systems use real truths preserved over time (God's Word) as guidance and are excited about the lives they will impact for the better through you!

CHALLENGE: Who do you look up to? Who inspires you? Why do they inspire you? What do they pursue above all else? Write down the patterns you see. And remember that for every leader, there's another person/passion guiding them behind the scenes. It may be God, or it may be something else.

THOUGHTS:

DAY 38

WHO YOU SURROUND YOURSELF WITH

1 Corinthians 5:11

But now I am writing to you that you must not associate with anyone who claims to be a brother or sister but is sexually immoral or greedy, an idolater or slanderer, a drunkard or swindler. Do not even eat with such people.

I f a friend "sticks closer than a brother" (Proverbs 18:24), then our lives can be influenced by who we hang around. If we want to walk with God in righteousness and truth, then our friends should have the same desires. Paul wrote to the city of Corinth to give them some incredibly helpful advice on friendship. His words encourage us to stay out of relationships with those who claim they are followers of Jesus but delight in sin on a regular basis.

Who do you spend most of your time with? Do their decisions make you proud to be their friend? Are you inspired by the person they are becoming? I used to believe it didn't matter who I hung out with as long as I spent time alone with Jesus. But with this mindset, I found myself starting to pattern my behaviors after those around me instead of the one who made me. I knew I needed new friends and needed to get out of the toxic relationship I was in at the time, but I wasn't surrounding myself with people who could encourage me to take the right steps in my life.

We all have roles in other people's lives. One of those roles should be to encourage them. It can be hard to do that when some around you are selfish and self-seeking. While some friendships are an opportunity to sew a seed of hope to those who do not know Christ, the friends in your close circle should be believers who can lift you up in prayer and call you out when they see you need it. The Word warns us to protect our hearts (Proverbs 4:23) because everything that we do flows from it. If we continue to let toxic people be the only voices in our lives, then toxic things will flow out of us too. Be encouraged that with fruitful friendships, you can be an encourager to others, and they can be the same for you as well.

TAKEAWAY: The way we spend our time on earth matters, and who we spend it with is equally important. God gives us guidelines because he loves and cares for us. He doesn't want us to be hurt by things we could have avoided with his guidance.

CHALLENGE: Examine your close circle of friends. Are certain friendships draining you? Take some time over the next couple days to examine your heart and the influence of those who surround you. If you do find that your friendship may be toxic, start praying over your friends and ask the Lord for some steps that may need to be taken in the near future.

THOUGHTS:

DAY 39

GOING FOR IT

Isaiah 43:18–19

Forget the former things; do not dwell on the past. See, I am doing a new thing! Now it springs up; do you not perceive it? I am making a way in the wilderness and streams in the wasteland.

I f I could preach one message to myself, it would be to stop holding myself back out of fear and "go for it." I don't know what "it" is for you. It could be a dream you've had on your heart for a while. It could be pursuing a relationship that would be incredibly fruitful for you and others, or it could be allowing yourself to try out for a certain sports team or a school play.

Whenever I find myself hesitant to do something I know I want to pursue, Shia LaBeouf's "Just Do It" video always pops into my head. (If you haven't seen his video, *please* look it up. You won't regret it.) "Just Do It" is also the slogan for a popular shoe brand, in part, I think, because we are often the ones who hold ourselves back from our biggest accomplishments and potential. Building up confidence can be a project when it comes to going for your dreams, especially when you feel that so much is at stake.

Reflecting on today's scripture, I'm reminded of how encouraging this passage of Isaiah is. So many motivational speakers will preach about "not dwelling on your past," and they're right! So many of us stay stuck in past failures and disappointments and don't pursue our dreams because we're afraid of failure. I'm going to give you the best piece of advice I've ever received, and it may sound a little crazy if you've never heard it before: Give yourself permission to fail. Failing is rarely as dramatic as we fear, and it can teach us the lessons we need to succeed in the end. God says he is making something new of you, your dreams included! Every day you are being made new, and every day God wants to use you. Even if you fail, there are new and wonderful things for you tomorrow!

TAKEAWAY: Go for that dream and surrender it to the Lord when you do! If he's put it on your heart, then it's worth pursuing and going down even the bumpiest of roads. He is making a way for you. Get excited and get started!

CHALLENGE: Write out your top 10 goals for the next year. Then write one dream you can get started on now. Start thinking and researching how you can begin working toward that goal.

THOUGHTS:

PURPOSE

Psalm 73:25–26

Whom have I in heaven but you? And earth has nothing I desire besides you. My flesh and my heart may fail, but God is the strength of my heart and my portion forever.

In Psalm 73, the writer of the psalm is praying to the Lord. He is overwhelmed by hurt and frustration because it seemed as if all the selfish, greedy, and evil people around prospered on earth. These people were prideful about what they had and who they were, and did not believe in God or want to respect him. The psalmist is tempted to continue to envy these people, but then he remembers that real and eternal joy comes from living according to God's purpose.

This psalm speaks to our main objective on earth. When we are tempted to stray away from our purpose and focus on others, we remember this psalm. Our number one purpose in life is to glorify God and delight in relationship with him (as highlighted in Psalm 73:28). However, pursuing this is often difficult because sin entered our world. Yet the message remains simple: it is only by restoring fellowship with God, through faith in Jesus Christ, that our purpose in life can be rediscovered.

So why does restored fellowship give us purpose? Only in a relationship with Jesus do we find our *true* purpose on earth, which is to love God and love others. It gives us fulfillment in a broken world. We were all created to glorify Jesus and enjoy eternity with him. We glorify God by fearing and obeying him, keeping our eyes on our future home in heaven, and knowing him intimately. Intimate knowledge of someone comes from walking with them. We enjoy life and enjoy our Father by following his intentions for us, which allows us to experience lasting and true joy. He desires this life of closeness and faith for all of us so that we can live life to the fullest.

A restored purpose keeps us from envying those around us, and we are left incredibly thankful for our lives because we *know* why we exist. There is no need to look to the left and right to compare what our friends or family are flourishing in to what we are doing, because our path is unique to our lives! In the end of our walk on earth, we want to hear, "Well done, good and faithful servant" from God. There will be sorrow, wretchedness, and evil around us in the meantime, but we can take comfort in the fact we play a part in God's ultimate plan for our world, one that includes justice and peace.

TAKEAWAY: When you are tempted to throw up your hands and give up, remember what you're fighting for: eternal joy, not temporary fun or prosperity. I'm sure we've all been frustrated at one point or another when we do the right thing yet seem stuck in our circumstances, and then see those who are behaving badly getting the very things we want (like fame, fortune, or the relationship of their dreams). There is a peace and beauty in knowing God intimately and following him above all else. What he can provide is greater than anything this earth has to offer.

CHALLENGE: Are there people or thought patterns present in your life that are holding you back from walking in your purpose? Do some self-examination and invite the Lord in to guide you to truth. Meditate on Psalm 73 and identify any similarities you see between today's world and the world in which this psalm was written.

THOUGHTS:

DAY 41

AN ATTENTIVE HEART

Luke 10:41–42

"Martha, Martha," the Lord answered, "you are worried and upset about many things, but few things are needed—or indeed only one. Mary has chosen what is better, and it will not be taken away from her."

We're always taught it's better to give than to receive, but sometimes that doesn't mean what we think. Which is why I love the story of Mary and Martha receiving Jesus into their home. Both wanted to honor Jesus, who'd raised their brother Lazarus from the dead[1], but their responses are different. Martha was worried about being a good host by serving their guests, while her sister, Mary, wanted to listen to everything Jesus had to say. Mary stepped back from helping her sister get things tidied up for Jesus and simply paid attention to him. Despite all the things she could be *doing* for Jesus in this moment, she believed Jesus' words were more important.

When Martha saw her sister wasn't helping, she complained to Jesus because she felt Mary was ignoring her work. In Luke 10:41–42, Jesus lovingly corrects Martha and the posture of her heart. He tells her that Mary in this instance receives the higher praise because she saw a rare opportunity to listen to him and knew his words would be valuable. In other words, Mary took the time to pay attention, while Martha let her busyness distract her.

But even though we know Mary chose better, it's still

---

1 If you haven't read the story of Lazarus yet, it's a must. So good.

easy to be like Martha, becoming wrapped up in "giving" by serving in the church and honoring God with our work—and then feeling angry at Marys for "receiving" too much by not pitching in/doing what we think God wants. When those emotions happen, we need to be understanding and not assume the person is doing something wrong, because they may be pointing us toward an important truth we're missing in our busyness.

Does your life reflect spending *time* with Jesus despite all the things you could be *doing*? Or are you more like Martha, who was impatient in this passage and concerned about getting the help from her sister, despite Jesus' presence?

Jesus is present with us, dwelling in the hearts he has saved with his extravagant display of love on the cross for us to look back on. Mary was so excited to listen and hang at Jesus' feet because she knew he was well worth her attention.

TAKEAWAY: Tune your heart toward attentiveness to the Holy Spirit. Oftentimes, we may believe that doing all the things *for* God is more important than sitting at his feet and being *with* him.

CHALLENGE: Today, I challenge you to ask God for a deep awareness of his presence while you serve others, and to look for the small and big ways the Lord is working in your life. It might help to jot a note in your phone as you go throughout the day. You'd be surprised just how intentionally God shows up for you.

THOUGHTS:

LISTENING FOR GOD'S GUIDANCE

Ephesians 4:14–15

*Then we will no longer be infants, tossed back
and forth by the waves, and blown here and there
by every wind of teaching and by the cunning
and craftiness of people in their deceitful
scheming. Instead, speaking the truth in love, we
will grow to become in every respect the mature
body of him who is the head, that is, Christ.*

To know if God is speaking to us, we need to be able to recognize his voice. God speaks in many ways, through many different people. But that doesn't mean we should listen to every voice we hear. The world is sinful, and so are the people in it. In a world that often wavers in what it believes, we must be attentive to the voice that comes from the rock in which we put our faith. Only then can we mature in our faith and grow to be more like Jesus, knowing what is godly and right.

When God speaks, his voice always agrees with his Word. If the voice you are listening to does not align with Scripture, it is not from God. His is not a voice of confusion, but one of loving direction. Get to know God by reading the Bible closely, and you'll get to know his voice. When he speaks, he will always guide you in a better direction—not necessarily what *you* think is best, but what will be for your greatest good in the long run. As our thoughts become more like his, we will be able to recognize the schemes of the enemy and fight against them.

If God's voice is present in his Word (because it is written by him and the people he chose to speak through), then his voice is just as active today as it was when the different books of the Bible were written. Want to know what he has to say about your decisions and lifestyle? It's written in his Word. As you get to know his voice, you'll notice when he speaks in other ways too, because the guidance and encouragement you receive from others will line up with what you already know from reading his Word. Pray that the Lord reveals what he wants you to hear through these people and expose things that are not of him.

TAKEAWAY: God's ways are better than ours; when we are in tune with what he has to say, we can accomplish big things and grow more confident in our faith. Standing firm in the Word of God, we learn to recognize the voice of our Father and filter out the voices of the world.

CHALLENGE: Start comparing the advice you hear from leaders, friends, and others in your circle of influence to the Word of God. If their opinions aren't in agreement with Scripture, think twice about taking the advice. Once you begin practicing this, you will become more aware of the Lord's presence and how he looks after you.

THOUGHTS:

DAY 43

USING YOUR GIFTS

1 Corinthians 12:4–6

There are different kinds of gifts, but the same Spirit distributes them. There are different kinds of service, but the same Lord. There are different kinds of working, but in all of them and in everyone it is the same God at work.

sn't it crazy that the creator of the universe thought we were all worthy of special gifts and abilities? Isn't it incredible that your weakness might become your greatest strength as you allow Jesus to work through you? We are all gifted in different ways to bring glory to God, but these gifts can also bring joy to ourselves and others in the process.

Each of us is born with specific, unique, and individual talents that were meant to bring glory to God. For example, my brother was born with a natural talent to play the piano. Of course, he needed to practice it to hone his natural ability. But once he did, he discovered something he loved and was great at. Our talents become evident as we grow and mature, as opportunities for their use or expression occur, and as our environment allows them to develop. It is possible that a person may never know what their natural talents are if they are never able to express them. So I'm always pushing myself to try new things. We'll never know what we're talented at otherwise!

Spiritual gifts go one step farther than talents—they are God-given abilities of a particular spiritual nature and/or a spiritual purpose. These are what 1 Corinthians 12 specifically talks about. These gifts may or may not overlap with natural talents or learned abilities. For example, a person may be born with an aptitude for teaching. He goes to college and learns the practical ins and outs of teaching subjects in school. This gives direction and boundaries to guide his natural talent. After his conversion and study of Scripture, he may discover that he has the spiritual gift of spiritual teaching—something that is more than his natural talent or learned ability. God enables him to both understand and present his Word with clarity, power, and authority, and amplifies his natural ability to teach. God can work powerfully and effectively through someone with the spiritual gift of teaching to help others understand the Word of God more readily!

Sometimes learning a new skill can reveal God-given talent. You'll never know what your spiritual gifts are if you don't explore! A lot of times, talents can become passions that fuel a fire within you to share your gifts to help, inspire, or encourage others.

TAKEAWAY: The Holy Spirit is gracious and gives us each unique gifts. Although some of us may be talented and gifted in similar ways, we all have something unique that only we can do because we have a God that made none of us exactly alike.

CHALLENGE: Do you know what you're naturally talented at? Do you know what spiritual gifts you have? If not, I encourage you to ask your friends or family what they recognize in you. You may have a gift you don't even recognize in yourself, or you may have one that you can continue to grow. Write down what your gifts and talents are and pray over them this week. Ask God to grow you into a great steward of your gifts and talents. He gave them to you for a reason!

THOUGHTS:

RELINQUISHING CONTROL TO GOD

Matthew 6:34

Therefore do not worry about tomorrow, for tomorrow will worry about itself. Each day has enough trouble of its own.

ontrol freak. That's how I used to describe myself. It's not a pleasant thing to be. It's important to be a hard worker and use what God has given you to do an excellent job at whatever you are doing, but how often are we crippled by anxiety over being perfect? How often do we allow God to take over versus making sure everything goes according to *our* plan?

Today I believe you can be set free from the "control freak" mindset. However, it does take effort. The first step is understanding that, right now, you are exactly where you are supposed to be; fearing the future takes away from your joy. Yes, there are things to do, people to see, and things to look forward to. But the author of tomorrow is not you.

I am often tempted to fall into the mindset that *I* can control my future. A lot of my worry comes from fear that I won't be able to afford certain things, whether it is this semester's college tuition or just a fun night out. I try to stay smart by budgeting, but oftentimes I still worry that I won't be able to pay my bills. God has come through over and over again, usually in a way that makes it clear that he is the one looking out for me. Money can be a stressful subject for anyone, but I'm learning that trusting the Lord means being wise with what he's given me and knowing that he'll come through for me when times get tough or circumstances don't seem to be going my way.

Remember the Lord's faithfulness in both your high and your low moments. Give yourself permission to let go during times of uncertainty so you can let God be God. It is a *good* thing to give the control to the Lord. Sometimes it's as easy as noticing that you're in control mode and choosing to let go by consciously and deliberately shifting into surrender.

TAKEAWAY: "Being in control" of your life is an illusion, because you are not the author of your tomorrow. Breathe. Remember the faithfulness of God in the past and how far he's gotten you. Trust that he is present no matter what you feel.

CHALLENGE: The next time you are tempted to stress out over whatever your current situation may be, try this breathing exercise. Breathe in slowly for seven counts, and then exhale for five counts. Repeat three times, and then say, "I'm letting God be God today." Claim that truth for yourself!

THOUGHTS:

OVERCOMING FAILURE

Job 14:1

Mortals, born of woman, are of few days and full of trouble.

What does failure look like to you? Have you ever felt like you've massively failed yourself or others around you? It's important to know that our journey never ends with a failed attempt to go after our dreams, the ending of a relationship or friendship, bad grades, or even getting fired from a job. Why? Well, because there's always the option to keep going or to try something new.

To fail occasionally is to be *human*. None of us were born perfect. But to be a "failure" is when we are defeated by failure, refusing to get up and try again. A lot of times Christians believe they should be immune to failure because they have a relationship with God (shouldn't God make everything work out okay since he loves us?), but sometimes God allows us to fail for his own reasons. It may be to teach us that we can't do much solely on our own and he wants to show us a new way!

In our verse for today, it says that we as humans are all "of few days and full of trouble." The verse points out that all of us, whether we are Christian or not, will encounter trouble while living in our fallen world. We should expect hard times in life. Failing allows us to see what we can change for the future and it helps us recognize that we need to lean on Jesus and allow him to be our strength in trying times.

I'm thankful for the opportunity to fail, because it allows me to pick myself up and try again. God has marked out a course for each of us, and he wants us to delight in him even when the road isn't easy. Sometimes our course includes failure. But when our eyes are fixed on the one who authors our future, he can give us strength in our weakness, which ultimately leads to victory.

TAKEAWAY: Life is going to come with trouble, but it is your choice to get back up or run away. Let Jesus come in and walk with you. All you need to do is take things one step at a time.

CHALLENGE: If you feel like you've tried to make things happen on your own but feel stuck, write about how you feel. Pray over your feelings and dreams and ask for God's intervention. Invite him to be your leader. Be encouraged that some of the greatest heroes failed before they succeeded. He's got this!

THOUGHTS:

DAY 46

DATING WITH INTENTION

Proverbs 22:1

A good name is more desirable than great riches; to be esteemed is better than silver or gold.

D ating in general isn't easy, and romantic relationships aren't for everyone (1 Corinthians 7:38), but many of us will date at some point in our lives. I strive to have God at the center of all my relationships, including romantic ones. I am not a perfect example of "the godliest girlfriend" by any means, but I do know that Scripture gives amazing foundational guidance. In fact, God's Word outlines the core principles of godliness, purity, and unconditional love as being essential to the life of a Christian.

The Bible also encourages us to look to godly people for further guidance. Let me pass on the wise advice I've received from married couples over the years. When I've had conversations about dating, a respect for one another is something that is usually brought up early on. A huge part of dating, or any relationship in general, is a respect for each other. Respect the goals, dreams, and passions of the person you are currently dating, and if God blesses you with a spouse (whether or not they end up being the same person) by being a person of your word. This gives the relationship the opportunity to mature and for each person to show respect by demonstrating integrity, moral character, and devotion to God.

Additionally, never assume the person you are dating definitely will be the person you end up marrying. Life can throw us unexpected curveballs, and maintaining a relationship's integrity means maintaining *your* integrity and ensuring you are pursuing the Lord above your desire to be in relationship with another human. With this principle in mind, I've been praying for my future husband since I was sixteen years old. Although I don't know if God will bless this desire I have for a husband, I still submit that desire to him. Every month, I take some time to write out different areas I pray my future husband grows in: character, wisdom, discernment, and love. While praying over those qualities, I also pray that I grow in them too.

Finally, encourage those you date to grow spiritually. The Bible encourages us to be in relationships where we are equally yoked, which means being of the same faith. Being in a relationship with someone who holds the same beliefs as you sets you up for success and gives you a sense of confidence that you are both on the same page on the important issues.

TAKEAWAY: Strive to date people who have the same intentions you do, and consciously invest in the spiritual growth and well-being of the other person.

CHALLENGE: Write out a list of qualities you desire to see yourself grow in and start praying over them. And if you have a desire to be married someday, submit that desire to the Lord through prayer as well. If you want to start a journal dedicated to this, you should! It's super cool to watch the list change over time.

THOUGHTS:

DAY 47

LIVING A PURE LIFE

Proverbs 4:23

Above all else, guard your heart, for everything you do flows from it.

Growing up in the church, I would frequently hear the pastor instruct us to have a "clean heart" or to be "pure in heart." I always wondered what it meant, why it was so important, and what this looked like in practice.

What I've learned over the years is that the condition of your heart is directly related to what you choose to let in. In Christian culture, it can be easy to judge ourselves based on what our different struggles and sins are. But Jesus encourages us to be better in our own lives every day by being cautious about what we read, view, and entertain.

Living this way takes intentionality and an awareness of who we desire to be in Christ. It is also important to mention that living a pure life does not simply mean sexual purity. Although that is an important part of living a pure life, it is not the main focus. What music do you listen to? What type of friends do you have? Do you spend more time on social media than is necessary? (Been there, done that.) Be careful what you entertain, because entertaining unhealthy things can grow unhealthy things in you if you continue to feed those desires. It is easy to give into greed, anger, selfishness, pride, discontent, and impatience. It is hard to keep our thoughts and actions pure, but it is entirely possible by setting healthy boundaries for ourselves and asking the Lord (our best advocate) for his aid. Christ has given us power and authority over our sin because he defeated it once and for all. As you strive for a pure heart, remember that you are not in it alone, and God is *proud* of you.

So, we've talked about living a pure life, but what does that exactly mean? Being pure in heart means you have a heart that is clean from sin—a heart that has been purified by the death and resurrection of Jesus on the cross—and one you desire to keep clean. Pursuing him is the only way to live an abundant life. Your sins have been forgiven and your slate is washed clean. This also means as we grow in him, our thoughts shift toward things that are honorable and loving; they should be less prideful, discontent, impatient, angry, and envious. Although we still do wrestle with our flesh, we have the opportunity to say no to unhealthy desires. These desires do not satisfy us, but Christ's desires for us always satisfy more than we'd ever dream of. Strive to be a person who pleases God, and your behaviors will reflect how God would want you to act. The only way to be pure in heart is to give your life to Jesus and ask him to cleanse you of your sins, and then walk in relationship with him. God is the only one who can make our hearts pure.

TAKEAWAY: The path of purity in all avenues of life is one worth traveling on. Sin is often disguised as pleasure at first, but it only leads to destruction. Choose to guard your heart, for the one who made you treasures you so much. He gives us instruction on how to live an abundant life full of lasting joy and happiness, so we should go out and walk in that light!

CHALLENGE: Write out Psalm 51:10 on a notecard and place it in a prominent spot for the next two weeks. Commit to memorizing it. Let this scripture be your prayer.

THOUGHTS:

DAY 48

JOY IN THE HARD TIMES

Romans 8:18

I consider that our present sufferings are not worth comparing with the glory that will be revealed in us.

Sometimes life can be tough. A family member passes away, your car breaks down, and you get a bad grade on a test—all within the same week! It's easy to get overwhelmed by it all. The truth is that life is full of heartbreak, loss, and hurt. But we are not alone in facing it. Your comforter is right beside you, and the pain you are experiencing right now cannot even compare to the joy that is coming. This earth is temporary, and so is your pain.

Hold on to peace and lean into what you are feeling, but allow the Lord to hold you while you do. Nothing surprises the Lord; he has it all planned out! Why worry about life when God has it all under control? Your book is already written, and he knows the ultimate ending. Have peace and know that Jesus has conquered death and overcome the world. There is nothing he cannot do.

Remember to rejoice. You may be thinking, "Rejoice? How can I rejoice when I feel like my world is falling apart? How can I rejoice when I feel so sad and alone?" When Paul and Silas were beaten and shackled in a dark cell, they began praying and singing praises to God. (Yes, *while* shackled and injured!) Other prisoners saw them praising God even in their misery, and they were astounded. Paul and Silas's praise to God in their darkest time showed the other prisoners just how much they loved and desired to be with their God. Having joy, even in the direst of circumstances, will show others that we trust God. Rejoice, because he is always there and will never leave us!

TAKEAWAY: You might be surprised at how God can work in your life when you surrender your pain and sorrow to him. He will open your eyes to the good in your life; he will put people in your life to uplift and encourage you; he will give you strength to get through every hardship you endure. Trust in him and cast your burdens on him because he cares so much for you.

CHALLENGE: Having joy in tough circumstances is possible. We are allowed to grieve loss and be frustrated by temporary difficulties, but, as Christians, we have a hope that others do not. Today, take some time to read Romans 8 and be encouraged by what God may be speaking into your life through this chapter.

THOUGHTS:

GOD'S PURPOSE FOR FRIENDSHIPS

Ecclesiastes 4:9–10

Two are better than one, because they have a good return for their labor: If either of them falls down, one can help the other up. But pity anyone who falls and has no one to help them up.

Knowing you have friends whom you can trust and know will be by your side no matter what is one of the best feelings in the world. In the past, I had trouble finding friends who would encourage me rather than tear me down. Although I wanted better friends, I actually had a lot to learn about being a good friend myself too.

Fortunately, throughout the years I've made some incredible friends who are consistent in character, living out who God has called them to be. Most of my friends don't live in the same state as me, yet our relationships are as strong as ever because we've invested in each other, and Christ is also at the center of their lives.

Ecclesiastes 4:9–10 mentions that two people together is better than one. Why? Because we need each other to help us up when we fall and to hold us accountable. Friends should be chosen carefully because, as Paul told the Corinthians, "Bad company corrupts good character" (1 Corinthians 15:33). If you are seeking out friends, make sure you are good company to be around as well. Desiring a righteous friendship but not working to be a good friend yourself is harmful and will result in bringing others down with you.

Good friends are hard to come by, so be a *great* friend. Stay away from gossip about others. The Lord's purpose for friendship is to lift each other up to him so that we live in joy! If someone is talking rudely about another person, and you consider them one of your friends, have nothing to do with it. Lovingly let them know that you want to build up those around you instead of tearing them down. Avoiding a toxic gossip habit and learning to turn away from rude talk will lead to friendships that will bless you and the other person!

Go to battle for your friends in prayer. If they had an awful day at work or school, be there as someone they can lean on. Be intentional about checking in on your friends, and love them in the way they like to receive love. Quality time, gifts, affirming words, or acts of service are all super fun ways to show your friends you care about them. Relationships take effort—that is what makes friendship beautiful! It can be messy (aren't all relationships) because we are flawed humans. But what an opportunity to share life with other people.

TAKEAWAY: None of us work better alone. Find ways to build up the friends you have or step out and be a friend to someone else.

CHALLENGE: Text the three people you feel closest to and let them know how much you love and appreciate them. Mention two things you like about them, and one thing that encourages you about them. Try to make this a habit once every week! Healthy friendships start with you!

THOUGHTS:

SHARING YOUR FAITH

2 Timothy 1:8

So do not be ashamed of the testimony about our Lord or of me his prisoner. Rather, join with me in suffering for the gospel, by the power of God.

In his second letter to Timothy, Paul encourages his mentee to stand firm in his faith, to remember God's past faithfulness through hard times, and to share the faith he has with others. Today, we can read this letter from Paul as encouragement for us to do the same.

You and I are called to live out our faith by sharing it with others. As a Christian, I can sometimes live out what I say (by being slow to anger, loving to strangers, giving to those in need) in public much easier than sharing the gospel. This is just an honest confession of mine, but I get scared to talk about the way Jesus has impacted my life because oftentimes I am afraid of rejection. However, despite our fears and emotions, we are called to share our hope with others. Because we have found the cure to death by eternal life through Jesus! It's like if we found the cure to cancer; we would want everyone to be healed of it.

So how do we become bold about sharing our faith? I found that being creative in sharing has encouraged me to share more. Whether it's writing a letter, sharing worship music, or going out of your way to radically love someone, you can find unique ways to expose others to the gospel message. When you provide people with hope while still leaving room for them to ask questions, you are extending an invitation for them to get to know Jesus better and seek him out. I know my faith has become stronger the more I've asked questions and sought out the answers.

TAKEAWAY: Have confidence in the faith you have, even if you have questions yourself. We can trust that in our seeking, more and more of God will be revealed to us and others. Let's share the hope we have with others!

CHALLENGE: Get creative with how you share Jesus with those you meet! Don't be afraid to have conversations with unbelievers even though you may not know all the answers. Be encouraged that God will work on their hearts. Today, I encourage you to start a conversation about Jesus with someone you know fairly well. This conversation doesn't have to be a preaching moment for you, but an opportunity to learn more about that other person's beliefs and to share your own faith! It might take some time, but build up a friendship based on the similarities you have with this person. You could be much more alike than you think! Then be willing to share the best news you've ever received.

THOUGHTS:

HOW TO BECOME MORE PRESENT

Isaiah 26:3

You will keep in perfect peace those whose minds are steadfast, because they trust in you.

Do you ever have trouble sleeping or paying attention because there are so many things going on in your mind? Do you find yourself constantly distracted? When was the last time you stopped to think about what you were doing and why?

In Isaiah, the prophet talks about being steadfast in the presence of God. No matter where we are or what we face, if we are present in our situations and set our hearts and minds on him, he will grant us peace. A mind focused on God is rewarded, but we can't be loyal to him if we aren't centered on where he has us right now.

When my focus and attention go to other peoples' lives—what they ate today or who they hung out with according to social media—I find myself lost in their world and not present in mine. To become more present where God has put me, I must focus on him first. Because I know social media presents a lot of temptations for me, I choose not to engage with it for the first three hours after I wake up. Instead, I immerse myself in God's Word, listen to music, or simply take some time to think before I tackle my day. When life is busier, I spend time praying in the shower or listening to music and reflecting on who God is to me.

So how do we become more present? By focusing on the

task at hand. Act in the now as best as you can for the glory of God. Although we may have huge to-do lists, identify what your priorities are, and then allow yourself to tackle them in their order of priority. If you are with a friend or coworker, be with that person and really listen to them instead of checking your phone or thinking about what else you have to do that day. A life of presence is one filled with intentionality, so gently remind yourself to be where God has placed you in that moment when you find yourself becoming distracted.

If you're at your job and you find yourself becoming overwhelmed, take a deep breath and remember why God has you there. Is he building your character? Giving you experience? Exposing you to new people/cultures? To become more present in your atmosphere, ask yourself these questions often. Your work matters, but your purpose and character matter more. How is God using this minute to shape you? Allow this new way of thinking to give you a new perspective on what you do in your day-to-day.

A practical way to remain present is to journal. I'll write just about anything in my journal. I'll even pull out my journal in the middle of the night to jot down random thoughts I have. Writing allows my thoughts to run clearly and ideas to flow uninterrupted. I recommend journaling about your fears, goals, dreams, sorrows, joys, what you are grateful for, what you are sorry for—anything that will help get the clutter out of your mind and onto your paper. This opens up more mental space for you to focus on the present moment.

TAKEAWAY: Be present in your own life and make God your top priority. By practicing mindfulness and focusing on him, he invites us to grow, personally and spiritually.

CHALLENGE: Did you know you can change your thoughts? Practice feeding your mind with presence. You can do this by listening to peaceful music, memorizing helpful scriptures, and laying aside distractions when need be.

THOUGHTS:

HOW TO NAVIGATE FRIENDSHIPS WHEN LIFE CHANGES

Ecclesiastes 3:1

There is a time for everything, and a season for every activity under the heavens.

’ve written about friendship several times throughout this book because relationships with others are incredibly important. Life is not meant to be lived alone. However, one constant in life is *change*; it's inevitable that things will not always stay as they are. Whether you're moving to a new area or starting a new job, a shift in life circumstances does not necessarily mean that your friendships have to change.

Seasons come and go, and so do some friends. But lasting friendships will endure the tough seasons of change or uncertainty. Just like a tree stands through winter, summer, spring, and fall, so should our relationships if they are rooted in God.

So how does a friendship endure changes or difficult times? Proverbs 18:24 says, "One who has unreliable friends soon comes to ruin, but there is a friend who sticks closer than a brother." To have lasting, reliable relationships, the Bible instructs us to walk with our friends through their hardships, be dependable, cultivate intentionality, and radically love each other. If a friend of yours has moved, reach out to that person and make it a priority to chat. What I have done over time is make a list of friends I want to call every week, and I call each one on certain days. It doesn't always work out this way, but at least there is a structure. Ideas like this show you prioritize your friends even if you aren't in close proximity.

TAKEAWAY: Times will change, and people will come and go, but there are a few godly friends who stick close through anything. Be the friend you want to have, and keep an understanding heart when life changes inevitably come.

CHALLENGE: Which friends are you closest to emotionally? Make time within the next two weeks to be present with them. Work on listening to hear them; don't respond with your own comments right away. Nourish the friendships God has blessed you with.

THOUGHTS:

BEING HONEST WITH THOSE YOU LOVE

1 John 3:18

Dear children, let us not love with words or speech but with actions and in truth.

Honesty is the best policy, right? It's not always the easiest road. There have been many times when someone's honesty has hurt my feelings. However, in the end, I am usually grateful the other person had the courage to speak truth. It's one thing to say we love and respect someone, but real and authentic relationships are built on being honest with each other even if a conversation may hurt the other person's feelings or change the dynamics of the relationship for a short while.

Real love requires honesty even when it may temporarily hurt. And while it is important to be honest, kindness is equally important. When I have had to confront a friend, I usually let them know I am being honest because I love them and want our relationship to continue and grow stronger. It is better to slightly inconvenience someone with the truth than let them endure a stretch of troubles. However, honesty is not an excuse to use unnecessarily harsh words. When I need to have a conversation like this with someone, I like to pause and reflect before deciding to move forward and confront the other person. We should think about our words, our tone, and our reasons for what we have to say.

Set up your conversations with the right intention. Let the person know you are coming to them out of love and concern over their decisions. Before you start your conversations, ask yourself if what you're about to say is kind, truthful, and honorable. This has guided me in many instances and helped me to make wise decisions about which conversations I should or shouldn't have.

TAKEAWAY: If we want a true faith in Jesus that isn't just talk, we must live out what we say! Encourage others along the way and lean on those who are striving toward the same goal. Speak the truth in love and hold honesty close to your heart.

CHALLENGE: Read 1 John 3. I'm praying that it will encourage you! Start praying for heavenly discernment.

THOUGHTS:

FAMILY RELATIONSHIPS

Ephesians 6:1–2

Children, obey your parents in the Lord, for this is right. "Honor your father and mother"—which is the first commandment with a promise.

Family relationships can sometimes be hard to navigate. It seems as if family members are often the easiest to get impatient with, start a fight with, or be selfish around. But God calls us to be different from our selfish impulses, even in our family. Our siblings can test our patience, parents can get into arguments, and spending time together can get difficult as we grow older. But whether we have blood-related family or others who have taken us under their wing, our call is to love and respect one another. That may sound simple, but I need to hear it every day.

My family has gone through a lot of changes. My dad was unemployed for a while, we've gone through several car crashes as a family, moved homes (and states), had many pets over the years, and the list goes on. But it's all brought us closer over time and helped us to understand each other on a deeper level. A great piece of advice I was given by a man at my home church was to pray for my parents. That's so simple. Though in order to pray for my parents, I had to know what was going on in their lives. So that encouraged me to be open with them, and they were open with me.

I was able to be a better sister to my siblings when I found out what they enjoyed doing with their friends and did that activity with them. My sister loves getting her nails done, so sometimes we bonded over acrylics and what was going on in her world. Family has taught me to become a better listener. I used to just talk so I could be heard, but now I can understand others, and be understood.

I don't know what your family looks like or what the dynamics are, but I do know that God loves family. I mean, he did create it! I encourage you to spend more time with the people you love, and if you live far away from each other, call them often. Let them know you love them by being obnoxiously encouraging. They might notice a shift in you and want to change some things for themselves!

TAKEAWAY: Family is not only important to us, but to God, who created it. Extending love toward those we grew up with, were raised by, or who have become family to us is an opportunity to embrace them and share the love of Jesus. Respecting parents, siblings, and extended family includes following the plan the Lord has for you. If your family isn't of the same faith as you, show them just how amazing your God is by the way you live and the conversations you have.

CHALLENGE: Hang out, write a letter, send a text, or call one of your family members (or a couple) today and thank them for being who they are. Encourage them with a quality you notice within them. Share a story and let them know you love them!

THOUGHTS:

USING YOUR MONEY WISELY

Matthew 6:19–21

Do not store up for yourselves treasures on earth, where moths and vermin destroy, and where thieves break in and steal. But store up for yourselves treasures in heaven, where moths and vermin do not destroy, and where thieves do not break in and steal. For where your treasure is, there your heart will be also.

As evangelical professor Bruce Waltke says, "Sinners love wealth and use people; saints love people and use wealth to help others."[1] Because Jesus gave his life for me, I can share my resources to help others and share more of him to the world.

Most people view money as the prominent stressor in life. It's even the leading cause of divorce! Believe it or not, trusting in Jesus will improve your money management. I've seen it in my life and in the lives of many others. Believing that God will come through when you need him is a matter of practice, but it is so freeing when you see him provide for you again and again. When you're not a slave to wealth, you can treat it correctly. If it's not your hope and security, you can use it as a tool. You can afford to lose money sometimes. You can risk giving it away or sharing it with others. You can put it to work so you can give more.

God's way of managing finances is countercultural. As Christians, we are called to higher standards in our lives, and that includes our financial lives as well; we shouldn't worry about how much money we spend, but we also should spend it carefully. And the balance is hard to find. Ever since

---

1   Bruce Waltke, *The Book of Proverbs Chapters 1–15* (Grand Rapids, MI: Eerdmans, 2004), page 193.

I moved out of my parents' house after high school, I became a saver. I wanted to avoid spending money at all costs, but I needed to learn balance (we all have to eat, right?). But I could have swung to the other extreme too. Society encourages us to sign up for several credit cards, purchase new cars we cannot afford, and live above what we can handle financially. But this is not a safe or a fun way to live. Instead of living a life spending only what we can afford, sometimes we end up owing money that we struggle to pay off for years.

We must be aware of two outcomes that could take root if we are not on guard and align our financial lives with God's Word: the spirit of poverty and the spirit of pride. Many people today believe wealth is evil and should be avoided at all costs. They have the spirit of poverty. Other people may struggle with the spirit of pride, which believes that wealth comes from (their) hard work alone. To combat both, we must nurture a spirit of gratitude instead. That means we display grace to ourselves and to others, focus on Jesus, and remember that our wealth ultimately comes from him. If we do everything out of gratitude for the monetary gifts he's given us, our acts from his generosity become gifts back to God.

TAKEAWAY: Remember that every good gift comes from God. Money can be good if used with the right attitude. Giving to others benefits the kingdom of God, and being wise with your money removes financial burdens that can often feel heavy.

CHALLENGE: Personally, I love listening to Dave Ramsey's podcast on financial advice. He is a Christian who has gone through bankruptcy, yet he was able to turn that low of his life and the lessons he's learned into a business that has blessed millions. I recommend you listen to his podcast, *The Dave Ramsey Show*—it's free!

THOUGHTS:

DAY 56

FINDING COMMUNITY

Hebrews 10:24–25

*And let us consider how we may spur one
another on toward love and good deeds,
not giving up meeting together, as some are
in the habit of doing, but encouraging one
another—and all the more as you see the Day
approaching.*

Community starts with you. Relationships start with your willingness to walk in the freedom that Christ has given you, while humbly pursuing others and extending grace. It takes work; friendships are not born overnight.

In Hebrews, we are instructed to encourage one another in love by continually meeting together. Community is what God has desired for us from the beginning of time. It is the gift of a rich and challenging life together, one that we need and can receive with joy. But how do we do this when moving to a new area or facing changes in our lives?

When moving to Atlanta in 2017, I knew I'd be lonely without friends. I asked my roommates where they went to church. One of them piped up and asked if I was in a small group. She knew some of her friends were starting one for people my age. What a God thing! I immediately got involved, and now some of these girls are my closest friends. There wasn't much to it other than showing up to gather with these girls. Learning about their dreams, changes, and the challenges in their lives makes me excited to have them as friends, and I don't know if I would be the same person without them.

What the writer of Hebrews meant when he encouraged us to "not give up meeting together" is to pursue friendship with each other on a consistent basis. When two or more are gathered in Jesus' name, his presence is there (Matthew 18:20) also. Showing up allows God to work in our lives and create community where there wouldn't be one otherwise.

TAKEAWAY: Having hands to hold through life makes all the difference. Encourage those close to you, and remember we are all flawed humans with an incredible God.

CHALLENGE: I challenge you to take a step toward love today by finding a community to be a part of. Do what you have to do to get plugged in! Ask your friends or people at church, or even search the internet to find ways to start investing in other people in your area. If you are already part of a small group, see if you can deepen your relationship with at least one person.

THOUGHTS:

STEPPING OUTSIDE YOUR COMFORT ZONE

2 Timothy 1:7

For the Spirit God gave us does not make us timid, but gives us power, love and self-discipline.

An ordinary life is *boring*. The hustle and bustle of what some people choose to hold their hope in is wavering ground. Temporary satisfaction in things on earth is not worth putting our hope in, because it is not eternal.

Alternately, living a life with Christ is exciting. But it can also be scary when we're given opportunities to try something we may not be skilled at yet or feel unqualified for. We tend to focus on the negatives rather than all the great things that could happen as a result of following Jesus into the adventure he has called us to. The very call on our lives is not a comfortable statement ("Then Jesus said to his disciples, 'Whoever wants to be my disciple must deny themselves and take up their cross and follow me.'" Matthew 16:24), but the Holy Spirit at work within us gives us all we need to be bold in our faith, work life, school, family, etc.

When was the last time you were challenged to do something out of your comfort zone? Did you follow through with it? Some of the most incredible friendships I have now were a result of me pushing past the introverted side of myself and engaging in a conversation with someone. I'm always thankful for those who have pushed me to be better by trying something new, saying yes to something I may be afraid of doing, all while knowing that God sees me, and he goes with me (and has gone before me). Opportunities to grow through taking a step with God into the uncomfortable are great—we just need to be on the lookout for them and start stepping.

TAKEAWAY: Growth often happens during uncomfortable times. Christ's power is at work within us if we are acting in the Holy Spirit and taking steps away from our usual routines. These opportunities can be challenging but usually result in a deeper understanding and appreciation of the God we serve.

CHALLENGE: Today I encourage you to recall anything you've done in the past year that has taken you out of your comfort zone. It could be embarking on a new friendship, starting a business, or making a small decision that led to even bolder ones. Whatever these instances are, write them down and evaluate where you are now. Are there any additional steps you need to take to walk into the adventurous calling God has for you?

THOUGHTS:

DAY 58

TAKING ADVANTAGE OF THE OPPORTUNITIES YOU HAVE

Ephesians 5:15–17

Be very careful, then, how you live—not as unwise but as wise, making the most of every opportunity, because the days are evil. Therefore do not be foolish, but understand what the Lord's will is.

We all have different talents and abilities; as a result, we are all presented with different opportunities. When Paul was writing to the church at Ephesus, he gave them a guide to follow to make the most of their days. Paul says to "[make] the most of every opportunity" and to be "children of light" (Ephesians 5:16 and 5:8). Down every path we walk on earth, we have the opportunity to share the light we have received through Christ. That is a gift in itself.

Don't miss out on your opportunities because you cannot see past your current situation or are too busy chasing someone else's dreams or living according to someone else's standard. It can be hard to focus on the path you're on when everyone seems to be doing "better" or going "faster" than you are, but don't lose heart. They are on their own path, and so are you. Don't let your opportunity pass because you are looking through the wrong door. Keep your eyes focused on the plan God has for you in your current circumstances. Say yes to chances to practice your gift and share the hope you have!

A big problem I see in people my age is a tendency to spend most of our time looking to what everyone else is doing and then get frustrated with where we're at. We don't see others' tears behind closed doors, or the fight they had to put up to make their dreams happen. The way to combat comparison is to praise others for what they accomplish. Who knows, there may even be an opportunity to be a part of what they are doing! If not, continue to be honest about where you're at with the Lord. He understands any frustrations and wants to show you the unique assignment he's given you on this earth! When an opportunity presents itself (through work, friends, school, etc.), pray for God to reveal if that is the way to go!

TAKEAWAY: We are blessed to have opportunities to be who we were created to be while walking with Jesus. The will of the Lord is to spread his name farther in every way possible. So, take chances and utilize the opportunities that present themselves to display the gifts God has given you.

CHALLENGE: Spend today writing down the opportunities you have right now. Also jot down how you express your passions. Through art? Sports? Music? Once you recognize the opportunities, gifts, and abilities you possess, think about how you can show love to people through these talents, and surrender the execution and timing to God.

THOUGHTS:

REACHING OUT TO THOSE DIFFERENT THAN YOU

Galatians 3:28

There is neither Jew nor Gentile, neither slave nor free, nor is there male or female, for you are all one in Christ Jesus.

n order to know the full love of God, we should become familiar with those who are different from us. We are all reflections of tiny pieces of God, so we should take advantage of the opportunities we have in our day-to-day lives to get to know more of who God is by being present with his people, each one unique in their own way!

In 1 Thessalonians, we are encouraged to help those who are weak and to be patient with everyone. (Yes, *everyone*.) And being patient can be exhausting sometimes. But keep in mind that the kingdom of God is open for every type of person to receive. Christ's family has been advanced through history by men and women, children and youth, people from many ethnic backgrounds, and people of many languages!

A big part of reaching out and sometimes being friends with those who are different from yourself is asking questions. Whether they grew up in another country, speak multiple languages, love some unique-to-you food, or just have had different experiences, get to know who they are and what makes them special. For me, I was always curious what my African American friends thought about racial issues, what hurts they've had in the past, and how I can be a better friend by understanding these things more. Many times, people want to talk about their hurts and frustrations. I think most people are just afraid to be awkward and make the first step. But we get to see more of who God is through his people by engaging with them in ways that could be awkward at times. You got this!

Sometimes it can feel as if we are so small and can't make a difference, but all of us can do our part to build one another up no matter who we are! Examine the circle around you. Is there uniqueness in others that you should celebrate? What can you do to learn from those who are different from you and probably have wisdom to share?

TAKEAWAY: Get to know people who are different than you. Extend a hand to someone in need. Give your time, money, and resources to others. All that we are given is a gift from the Lord anyway, so why not share what we have?

CHALLENGE: One of the biggest groups in need is the homeless. Think about how someone's life could be changed/improved if you gave away something that you just don't use! I encourage you to visit your local homeless shelter soon to give a few things away. It might be outside of your comfort zone, but these people are just like you and me.

THOUGHTS:

REMOVING LABELS

Genesis 1:26

Then God said, "Let us make mankind in our image, in our likeness, so that they may rule over the fish in the sea and the birds in the sky, over the livestock and all the wild animals, and over all the creatures that move along the ground."

Oftentimes, the world places labels on things that shine differently than others. I mean, sometimes we put labels on ourselves too. We all have certain aspects that make us who we are. These unique qualities are what make us "shine" apart from others. The labels we give ourselves usually show which lens we choose to operate in. For example: Someone who operates from fear can make choices that never challenge them or allow them to seize new opportunities. I was fearful I wasn't good enough to complete a class that was extra hard for me, so I did everything I could to get a good grade. But I ended up barely passing, because unhealthy fear was my motivation.

When God created each of us in the beginning, he said, "Let us make mankind in our image" Meaning that you and I were created in the likeness of God! What if we chose to live our lives out of that lens?

What God didn't say is, "Let us create people who are fearful of the future, of other people on earth, and are also shameful beings." If he did I wouldn't be writing this book! God looked at the earth and all that was in it and decided it would be even more incredible with you in it. Try to think about that for a second. All the lies you've been told and rude things you have been called in your life are not true in the eyes of God. In order for me to free myself from the rude comments I've gotten over the years (example: "Your face is chubby, and your voice is annoying."), I had to go back and remember *who* told me. Then I told myself: "Is (insert person's name) God? Nope. They were not given authority to tell me who I am!"

If you're laughing (or cringing) right now, I don't blame you. But there is power in what you tell yourself, especially after someone tries to claim a lie is true.

To live above all else with the one who created you, you must know who you are to him. I mean, truly his thoughts are higher and 100 percent accurate of us. How cool is it to know that the true God we are in relationship with wants us to know what he thinks of us?

TAKEAWAY: It's not easy to believe who God says we are and that we are made in his image. But since it is truth, it is important that we take it in! You were created by God and to live in joy.

CHALLENGE: How do you see the world? What fears do you have? These are just a few questions to get you writing today. Ask the Lord to intervene where you are seeing unclearly.

THOUGHTS:

BIBLE STUDY GUIDE

Here is a mini topical guide for some books of the Bible to study as soon as you can.

Genesis . . . . The beginning

Exodus . . . . Deliverance

Ruth . . . . Wholehearted redemption

Job . . . . Blessings through intense suffering

Psalms . . . . Praise in storms and the good times

Song of Songs . . . . The ultimate love and marriage guide

Matthew . . . . The kingdom of God

James . . . . Sincere faith

1 Peter . . . . Responding to suffering

2 Peter . . . . Warning against false teachers

Revelation . . . . The unveiling of Jesus Christ

ACKNOWLEDGMENTS

There are so many people who have shaped this devotional into what it is, and I have so much gratitude for each and every one of you.

My family—Mom, Dad, Chandler, Kylie, you encouraged me to write more books since the time of *Your Own Beautiful*. Without your support, I don't think I'd be writing this! I love you all so much.

Nicholas Hurst—As I write this, we are engaged! When this book comes out, you'll be my husband. There is no one else I'd rather do life with. Thank you for instilling love and encouragement into me on a daily basis. We're better together.

Cassie Hanjian—I can't say enough good things about you, Cass! You've helped me achieve the goals I've set for myself as an author, and you push me to be a better writer every day. Thank you for being who you are and for your support as my agent. It's been so fun to be engaged at the same time as you!

The Zondervan team—Thank you to Annette Bourland,

Sara Bierling, Londa Alderink, Jennifer Hoff, Jacque Alberta, and the many others who helped make this devotional a reality. My apologies for having to deal with my opinionated brain, but my upmost love to each of you for your expertise and love for this book. You guys are amazing at what you do, and I am so thankful to work with you!

To those who wrote endorsements—Thank you for believing in the vision that God has given me for this book! You've inspired me so much, and I cannot thank you enough for believing in the work God wants to do through me.